By Colin M. Turnbull

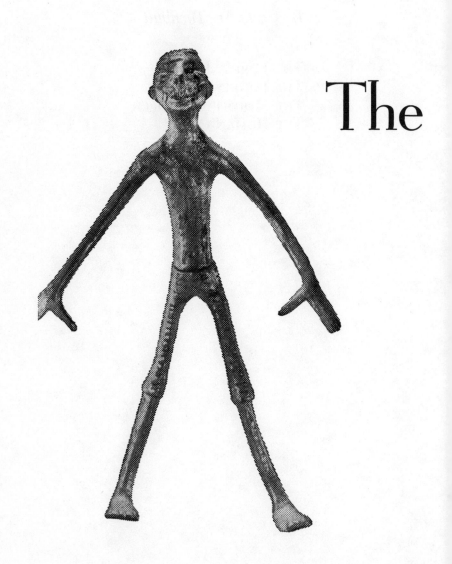

The

Colin M. Turnbull

Lonely African

A TOUCHSTONE BOOK
Published by Simon & Schuster, Inc.
NEW YORK

This Touchstone Edition, 1987

Published by Simon & Schuster, Inc.
Simon & Schuster Building
Rockefeller Center
1230 Avenue of the Americas
New York, NY 10020

TOUCHSTONE and colophon is a registered trademark
of Simon & Schuster, Inc.

Manufactured in the United States of America

10 9 8 7 6 5 4 3 2   Pbk.

Turnbull, Colin M.
   The lonely African.
   (A Touchstone book)
   1. Africa, Sub-Saharan—Social conditions.
2. Acculturation—Africa, Sub-Saharan. 3. Culture
conflict—Africa, Sub-Saharan. 4. Detribalization.
I. Title.
[HN773.5.T88   1987]   306'.0967   87-4751
ISBN 0-671-64101-8 Pbk.

Contents

Contents

Introduction

There has been much said and written about Africa's emergence into our brave new world of the atom bomb, power politics, cutthroat economics and mutually exclusive ideologies. The problems of Africa's emergence have been stated in terms of politics and economics, and the African's biological, intellectual and social potentialities have been discussed endlessly.

It has been generally assumed that whether or not the African is biologically our equal, increasing power is going to pass into his hands; and when it does, it is simply for him to decide whether he is going to throw in his lot with this bloc or that, accept economic aid from one nation or another, become Christian, Muslim, or atheist . . . it being almost inconceivable that he could decide to remain "native" and pagan. It is merely a question of a decision, and of whether or not the African is capable of making it intelligently. The alternatives he has to choose among are clear enough in our minds. About them there can be no question.

But these arguments have all been from our point of view; little thought has been given to that of the African. We have done our best to ignore the possibility that he might not be interested in blocs, that he does not necessarily think very highly of our version of democracy, nor of our highly exclusive, sectarian religion. And we have certainly ignored the possibility that our much vaunted notion of freedom, with all its economic and political apron strings, is too similar, for him, to the yoke of colonialism that he is still struggling to cast away. Nor has much consideration been given to the very deep personal problems that every individual African has to face in this period of transition, to the fact that the African has behind him an ancient and firmly established tradition, a way of thinking as well as of living, which he can not, even if he wants to, throw aside overnight in favor of what we have to offer in its place, however convenient it might be for us and for our conscience.

This book shows how the problems of transition reach down into the very depths of African society, into the souls of individuals, creating conflict and loneliness in all but a lucky few. If only we could understand this personal problem we might be able to understand the other problems more clearly and offer help more intelligently and in a way that would appear, at least, to be a little less self-centered. It might also be more acceptable to the African people.

In changing his mode of life, or having it changed for him, what kind of personal problems—problems of belief and faith, of values —does the African face? How does it affect his life and thought as an individual? That is what we try to discover here, in part. But there are two distinct aspects, for the situation is different in the urban and in the rural communities of Africa. In the towns and cities the overall problem is largely one of trying to think and act like a nation, of trying to forget tribal differences. For the individual it is more a problem of trying to reconcile a hard-dying tribal conscience with a nontribal *fait accompli,* of finding some means for justifying the new way of life that has been forced upon him.

In the rural areas, however, the tribal norm is much stronger, not yet having been driven underground, and the way of life is equally tribal, so there is no inner conflict. Nor yet are many troubled with the overall problem, for *nation* is still, in many areas, a foreign, meaningless term; the tribe is to them what the nation is to us, and the artificial boundaries drawn by colonial powers, often linking hostile tribes together and separating friendly ones, sometimes cutting a single tribe in two, mean nothing to the tribal African. They are dots of ink on a map, and that is all. His horizons are still those of the tribe, as are his ways and his thoughts. But nonetheless, transition is reaching him inevitably, if slowly. His problem is a different one, because while the urban African has had his way of life changed by the sheer force of circumstance, the rural African still has a certain element of choice—he has to make the decision for himself. It is not a question of finding an excuse or a compromise, it is a question of deciding between the old and the new in a context in which the old is still dominant but the new is plainly more powerful. His mind and soul belong to the one, his body increasingly to the other. He has a decision to make far more profound than that of his urban fellow, and it is a decision that is ultimately of far greater significance than which political or economic bias his leaders choose to adopt. His problem concerns the very soul of the people, their hopes and fears, their feelings and emotions, their friendship and their hatred.

To try and show both sides of the picture, in sketch form, each initial chapter deals with a certain aspect of the overall problem of transition in general, but with specific reference to urban communities, and is followed by a chapter that is in effect a biography of a member of a village in the eastern Congo, at a time when it was still under Belgian rule. The village is only a small cross section of a small tribe, but the story it tells has much that would apply to almost any African village, for everywhere the people are facing the same problem: which way can they turn?

In this way the different nature of the two sets of problems emerges, as does the basic similarity—that in both cases there is a void in the life of the African, a spiritual emptiness, divorced as he is from each world, standing in between, torn in both directions. To go forward is to abandon the past in which the roots of his being have their nourishment; to go backward is to cut himself off from the future, for there is no doubt about where the future lies.

The African has been taught to abandon his old ways, yet he is not accepted in the new world even when he has mastered its ways. There seems to be no bridge, and this is the source of his terrible loneliness.

C.M.T.

New York, 1962

1

Something New

It may be unnecessary to point out that Africa is not one vast jungle, infested with animals and savages, but it *is* worth pointing out the immense geographical diversity of the African continent, a diversity matched by an equal diversity of peoples and cultures. The tropical rain forest covers only a part of the western and central region; the north, with the exception of the Mediterranean fringe, is desert. The east and south consist largely of rolling, open grasslands rising to chilly heights, and, in places, to snow-capped mountain ranges.

This geographical diversity is at least as great as, if not greater than, that of Europe; yet when we think of Europe we do not think of a single people, and still less should we do so when we think of Africa. There are Arabs, Negroes, Nilotics, Bantu, Asians, and an extraordinary miscellany of Europeans whose contact with Africa has been over a much longer period than is generally thought, and many of whom are descended from people who settled there many generations ago. In this latter respect it is as well to remember, though it is incidental to our story, that the white South African entered that country from the south at the same time the Bantu were invading from the north, and so in temporal terms have equal rights there with the Bantu. The Bushmen, who were the unfortunate occupants of the territory at that time, were decimated and driven into the least desirable areas of the country by both invaders, in much the same way as was the American Indian.

There is, then, a complex multiplicity of peoples, languages and beliefs, and a long tradition of tribal migrations, wars, and contact with the outside world. Well before the Portuguese mariners established trading and victualing stations all around the coast in the sixteenth century, the Greeks and Romans had been acquainted with the continent, and the Romans had extended their empire all along its northern shore. But it was the necessity for supply points for ships trading with the Orient that brought the first shadow of western civilization to Africa south of the Sahara. For a time it was confined to the coastal area, since the coastal forest and the lack of navigable rivers make inland penetration all but impossible. But as the trade centers became increasingly important and populous the need for expansion of the authority and power of the traders became imperative.

The west coast, where the most important trading posts were first established, has had the longest and most profound contact of this kind, and today the west coast is lined with modern cities, the African inhabitants of which speak English or French or Portuguese as readily as they do their native tongues, sometimes more readily. And in the last few years modern cities have sprung up even in the heart of the continent, standing where the nineteenth-century explorers had found nothing but primeval forest.

In cities such as these the westerner can live just as though he were at home in his native country, performing the same acts, eating the same food, thinking the same thoughts, holding to the same ideals. To the casual observer the Africans in such urban centers are as western as the Europeans. They dress the same way, talk the same language, take part in the same economic life, and latterly even participate in the social and political life of the community. But the Europeans are more at home in these African cities than the Africans themselves. The African is a stranger on his own land; he knows it, and the Europeans know it.

East Africa was settled very much later, but settlement came with far more vigor and rapidity than it ever did on the west coast, and today the same kind of ugly, foreign towns and cities stand up in the middle of the East and Central African countryside, monuments to the fact that western civilization has arrived, and has come to stay. These glaring, garish cities have a defiant air of permanence, and of total disregard for their surroundings, that nicely reflects the attitude of their white builders and inhabitants.

In themselves these cities have brought a change in the way of life of the Africans who choose, or who become obliged by circumstance, to live there. There are many who choose, but equally many who have no alternative, either because the city is built on the land they farmed or that their cattle grazed, or because their own traditional way of life is forbidden them or made impossible by restrictive legislation. But both react to their new surroundings in similar ways. They are impressed by the superficialities, and they imitate them, sometimes slavishly, sometimes with charming variations (often founded in an appreciation of the inaptitude of the inelastic Western way) which the Europeans deride with smug satisfaction. "I've actually got a farm hand who wears a tie—but the stupid bastard doesn't realize you don't wear a tie without a shirt!" But the farm hand placidly continues to wear the tie, because it makes a bright splash of color, and is useful for tying up bundles, and refuses to wear the shirt that collects dirt and sweat and makes the Europeans smell so bad.

The superficial adoption of his culture by the African is what the European notices with pride, and is the yardstick by which he measures the African's progress towards civilization. He has been all too unaware of the more significant changes. The fact, for instance, that an urban life not only entirely disrupts the traditional family life of the African, but destroys all the practical economic and political ties that are of any significance to him, resulting in moral and spiritual degeneration. He is also naively unaware of the tremendous intensity of feeling generated by social segregation. The European, particularly in eastern, central and southern Africa thinks of African hostility and opposition as being founded entirely in political causes. He is so obsessed by the notion that the African wants political equality and equality of economic opportunity, thus challenging white political and economic supremacy, that he has failed to see that a great proportion of the real hostility, the real bitterness and hatred, springs from other causes, trivial to the Europeans but of deepest significance to the African.

To the European it is merely convenient to have separate eating facilities, separate traveling facilities, in fact separation wherever possible so that there is no need to meet the African socially. He does not think of it as insulting or degrading to the African, and he justifies it by saying that the African facilities are just as good as those for the European, though this is by no means always true. But to the African this separation *is* degrading, and the African has every bit as much pride and self-respect as the Europeans. But even more he resents it when he has acquired, with considerable difficulty because of the educational system, an education that is often far above that of the majority of the Europeans around him. He has accepted the need to prove himself their equal, and when he has proved it he naturally resents their blind refusal to acknowledge the fact, and comes to the reasonable conclusion that as far as the whites are concerned white supremacy has come to stay. And above all he resents the various ways in which opportunities are denied.

Edward, from Northern Rhodesia, was one of the brightest students at the London University Institute of Education. Most of us who were there studying the specific problems of colonial education were fired by something more than just enthusiasm; there was something about the course that was challenging. It demanded that first and foremost we try to understand the people among whom we were to work, their problems and their way of life and thought. It emphasized that we should understand without passing judgment.

It was a course that appealed to those with ideals, and perhaps it was the tremendous ideals burning in Edward that made him stand out. His one dream was to do well in his studies and return to his country to help in the overwhelming problem of education there. First and foremost, he wanted to fit himself to help, only secondarily did he want to prove to the white settlers and administrators that an African was capable of this kind of work. Edward and I became close friends, and we talked of these things many times.

A few years later when we both found ourselves in London I tried to contact him, not having seen him since we had left the Institute. There was no response. Eventually I met him at a political meeting and asked him why he had not replied to my letters or at least come around for a drink. He said, "Colin, I have come to the point where I can not trust any white man any longer, where I wish to have nothing to do with them—even my old friends."

He had returned to Northern Rhodesia with every qualification for a responsible post in the education department, and had been offered instead a job as teacher in a rural primary school. Administrative posts and higher teaching posts were for Europeans only. Africans were not considered fit for responsibility even if they did somehow manage to pass examinations that their white superiors had failed.

Today Edward, the quiet, gentle, easygoing student who was once fired with enthusiasm to work for his people alongside the British white settlers who had indirectly given him the opportunity for his education, and for whom he once had a considerable respect, is one of the most bitter men in Africa, feeling he can trust no white man simply because he is white. He is also one of the most violent antiwhite political agitators.

Edward's case is by no means exceptional. In fact it is difficult to think of any of the Africans whom I knew at the University in England who did not have their enthusiasm soured in this way. They came to England as young men who were aware that they were infinitely more fortunate than most of their fellows whose education was forever confined to the limits of a small, understaffed, unqualified, overcrowded, strictly segregated mission school leading to a doubtful high school level at the most. They lived in England relatively free from the social barriers that prevented any interracial contact in their homeland, and came to accept this as normal. One I know, who became one of the most successful law students to be called to the bar, was positively pro-British by the time he took a plane back to Kenya. When I met him later he described his plane trip, and how all the way he could not sleep, he was so full of the responsibility he felt he carried as one of the pitiful handful of Kenya Africans who had had such an opportunity.

"Then when we reached the airport at Nairobi," he told me, "the white man who had been sitting beside me, talking with me, eating with me, sharing the same lavatory, said goodbye. I got out of the plane and was faced by three lines for customs and immigration—one for Europeans, one for Asians, and one for Africans. And after I had gone through immigration, it having been noted that I was Kikuyu and therefore suspect and liable to restrictions of various kinds, I realized that here, in my own land, I was not even considered fit to piss in the same urinal as a white man."

These examples are typical of the experiences shared by Africans from East and Central Africa. It is here, together with South Africa, where racial intolerance has grown to almost ungovernable limits of fear and hatred through ignorance and stupidity. It is largely because in this part of Africa the European has made his permanent home, alienating land that once belonged to the Africans, often under very dubious pretexts; sometimes by deceit, sometimes by force. It is in this part of Africa where people have learned to hate each other to such an extent that any peaceful solution seems impossible.

Here the Kikuyu once farmed the rich and pleasant land of the

Kenya Highlands, and where they accepted pieces of paper from the first white men in exchange, they thought, for giving the white men permission to till the unused soil and take its fruits. But the white man thought in different terms. From his point of view the land had been paid for and bought and it was his to do with what he liked . . . and what he liked was to turn off all the Kikuyu "squatters" and keep his land for himself. What he failed to realize was the tremendously deep ritual attachment of the people to their land, the land of their ancestors. The Kikuyu in turn were unable to conceive of any sacrilege as great as the stealing of land in this way. To fight for it, yes, and let the stronger win; there was no shame in that. But to be tricked out of one's land, to be forced to give it up for all time without fighting, that was a disgrace difficult to live down.

Then when the Kikuyu had it explained to them that the white man considered their farming methods wasteful, and that this was an additional reason for taking the good farming land away from them, the Kikuyu reasonably asked to be taught better farming methods so that they could claim their land back. But even this was denied them, and acres of land went unused, adding to the ferment that led to Mau Mau. The deceit was too apparent; even the African could see that the white man was simply determined to take the best of what was going and to keep it. It was only the European who could not see through his own transparency.

And so, in East, Central and South Africa, the African has learned not only to hate, but also to despise the white man for his hypocrisy. For one of the characteristics of the African here is his honesty of thought and action . . . at least it was, until he learned differently. For instance, there is something illogical, to say the least, about segregation in a church that preaches the brotherhood of man, and there is something painful, to the African, about an old and highly respected white lady who was held in contempt by other whites because she insisted on her black servants accompanying her to church, even sitting in the same pew, and on one memorable occasion even drinking Communion wine from the same chalice. To the majority of the lesser breed of European the old lady was a degenerate aristocrat who was so far behind the times as to be a menace. To the Africans she was one bright but ineffectual spark in a cold ocean of hypocrisy.

In the British territories of East and Central Africa, where the stated policy is to progressively lead the Africans to self-government, the accusation of hypocrisy is particularly strong and bitter. Latter-day movements toward some form of political liberties for Africans have come too late, and with too much obvious reluctance to change this opinion. And it is a sad comment on the white population of these territories that so many thousands of Africans should have left, and are continuing to leave, and migrate into South Africa, despite its notorious reputation for apartheid. But there, say these Africans, they are paid better, they have schools and universities that they do not have in the British territories, better housing and labor conditions, and above all (this is a bitter pill), they say, "The white South African is honest. Discrimination is no worse, and at least we know exactly where we stand." However much the African may dislike discrimination he is big enough to respect honesty, and that is something he has not found very often in British East and Central Africa.

This may seem to be a one-sided picture, and indeed it is, but it is no less one-sided than the actuality, and it is certainly no more one-sided than the picture painted by the protagonists of the white man's "civilizing" mission in Africa. There are many settlers and administrators who feel that they are accomplishing some kind of God-given task, and there are many who have the interests of the Africans very much at heart—but there are few who put those interests on anywhere near the same level as their own. The number of those who are determinedly there for their own gain and who deliberately maintain racial inequality to insure their own economic and political supremacy was originally small, but is, if anything, apparently on the increase. But even these people condemn themselves out of their own mouths. There is one remark that can be heard almost anywhere in Kenya, and elsewhere, and from almost any type of settler, including men and women who have grown up there, who have been born there, and who are the proud possessors of the White Highlands. They are people who would never for a moment doubt their God-given superiority over the blacks, nor the right to possess their land. But with surprising frequency you can hear them assert that they would never employ Christian "boys," because they are so unreliable; they lie and steal and cause trouble. These diehard settlers prefer to draw their staff "from the bush," where "the native is unspoiled." This is an adequate comment on the effect of white civilization in anyone's eyes, but particularly in the eyes of the African.

And the tragedy is that until the end of the last war there was a great feeling of good will for the mother country and for the crown among all the British East and Central Africans, and even in South Africa. They recognized the potential good that could arise from a meeting of the two worlds. But something came into their lives at that point to sour the good will, to turn it rancid and unwholesome, finally to destroy it. Only the fragments of that good will remain, and only where civilization, as we know it, has had the least effect. The turning point was probably the realization that the meeting of the two worlds was not going to lead to a union of mutual benefit through cooperation and mutual respect, but was going to involve the total destruction of everything of importance to the African, including his beliefs, and result in a world primarily designed to benefit the whites, and only incidentally perhaps the Africans.

This was manifest in the increasing lack of respect for the African (such as the giving of preferential treatment to "black" foreigners, i.e., Asians, over the native Africans), which resulted in turn from a complete lack of any attempt to understand him. In default of understanding there can be no respect. The African, on the other hand, understands us all too well, and sees little reason for respecting us. Following the war there was heavy immigration of white men and women, many of whom were people who could never have held down a decent job in their own country, but who were welcome in East Africa simply because they helped to swell the white population. The country became filled with a class of people who had little idea of how to behave toward one another, let alone toward anyone else. They suddenly found themselves with large houses, motor cars and servants. But they were not up to the part, and their behavior in itself was enough to destroy whatever respect the Africans might still have felt for the British at that point. It is a common joke among Europeans in Africa to ask, "Are you married or do you live in Kenya?" for such are the moral standards among Kenya whites. A good-natured villager once said to me, "We have several wives, and we are faithful to them all, and we care for all their children until we die. You people can not even be faithful to one wife, and your children are such a nuisance to you that you send them away from home almost as soon as they can walk."

If the uneducated villager finds fault with us so easily, and with good justification, how much easier it is for the educated African living in urban communities. There, in everyday life, he comes in contact with the deceit that is synonymous with politics, but is often labeled "diplomacy," and with the mutual slaughter that is called a competitive economy, and with the farce (by our own stated standards as well as by African standards, let us note) that we call "family life," with nobody knowing or particularly caring who is sleeping with whom, because the children are all safely away at school in England anyway. And in the midst of this great center of civilization in heathen Africa the church (one for each denomination) raises its steeple and calls the faithful, the God-respecting,

to worship—white this side, black that—or, better still, it calls
them at separate times, or even gives them, with Christian gener-
osity, separate buildings so that nobody can accuse them of discrimination. We really have not given the African much to respect us for—except possibly the drugs to cure the syphilis we
brought with us.

In West Africa the situation is very different, and this difference
must be emphasized to avoid any unthinking generalizations about
Africa and its problems. For one thing, in West Africa there has
never been any settler problem. They say that the mosquito is their
best friend, because it prevented the white man from even wanting
to settle there. Even the political domination of the white man is
totally different in character, because there is not the same basic
problem of land alienation. Few white men choose to live their lives
in West Africa, and if they do it is more likely to be in the towns
and cities, rather than on vast private farming estates. Also, the
west of Africa has been in contact with the Europeans over a much
longer time than has the east or the south.

It is in the cities of West Africa that the reaction of the African
to western civilization is most significant. In the east and in the
south and in Central Africa, his reaction is understandably antago-
nistic. Where the settler is hostile, in his thought as well as in the
act of land alienation, the African is also hostile; where the settler
fears African economic competition the African fears economic sup-
pression; where the settler fears political equality the African fears
subjugation. But in West Africa there has been little hostility. Economic opportunity and political equality have come steadily and
relatively easily; together with opportunity for education the African has been given the opportunity to use his education to his full-
est capability in an unsegregated world. Certainly there has been
social segregation, but it *has* been social rather than racial. And
above all the African has been in close contact with the European

since the sixteenth century, and has had ample time to learn his ways.

Under these circumstances the conflict felt by the sophisticated, educated urban African can be seen more clearly than it can in the east, with its undercurrent of violent emotions. A man like Kwame Nkrumah is an excellent example. I met him in 1954, in Ghana, when the country was having its first general elections, and when Nkrumah was the virtually undisputed leader of all his people. It was almost entirely through his struggles and sufferings that Ghana won independence when it did.

Nkrumah not only had a wide education, in his country and elsewhere, but he had also traveled widely and seen something of different political ideologies in practice. With the double advantage of a British and an American education, and of travel, Nkrumah was, like many West Africans, perfectly at home in the western world—so long as he was not in West Africa. In his own country he was compelled to be more African than was, perhaps, his nature. And not entirely, I suspect, from the obvious political motives. In our informal discussions I got the impression that he felt a very real divorce from the people he was leading, because by virtue of his education he was less African than they. There were moments when he was positively impatient of their clinging to what he, like many other sophisticated urban Africans, called "savage superstition." And at times he was ashamed of them and would gloss over a discussion of traditional customs and beliefs as though they did not exist in this enlightened age. Yet he was sufficiently African himself to maintain a strictly African sense of time, breaking engagements or turning up early or late at will, and often showing a manifest respect for the more formal traditions.

The conflict appeared in other ways, such as the way in which he addressed political rallies in the heart of the capital, Accra, with all the paraphernalia of a modern public meeting, dressed in simple native clothes, or sometimes in imitation of the prison garb that stood as a symbol of the new-found freedom. On such occasions he would be borne through the streets of Accra on a great palanquin, and wherever he moved he would be sheltered by brightly colored umbrellas—a traditional Ghanaian symbol of status. Yet I have seen the same man, a day later, in the heart of the countryside, surrounded by traditional chiefs and nobles all in their traditional costume, but he himself wearing a well-tailored western suit.

Nkrumah expressed to me his admiration for Mahatma Gandhi, and I saw in it something of the same wistful admiration that Nehru had for the Mahatma. For Nehru, like Nkrumah, is divorced from his people by his own western education. Both men see in Gandhi a man who was never torn away from his roots, despite his many years in South Africa. They see a man who was able to look western civilization in the face, accept the good and condemn the bad, and do the same with his own culture. And both men see in Gandhi a man who could talk to the people, to the farmers and the peasants, and who could reach their hearts.

Wearing traditional dress will not make Nkrumah more African any more than his tailored suits make him European, and this is the case with most urban Africans. In a way it is easier for them to live in Europe than it is back in their own homeland, and I have seen the same people in both surroundings. In Europe they can live in the way they have been taught, and dress and talk in the western manner without the fear of being made to feel conspicuous by suddenly meeting a traditionally arrayed kinsman. And away from their native soil its power is not so great over their minds and souls. But however westernized they may seem in Europe, back in Africa there is a hidden force that pulls them the other way . . . the irresistible weight of centuries of tradition. This is the conflict that they have to face. Their way of life has been irrevocably changed, but not their spirit.

There are some who openly compromise, and perhaps they are the happiest. But to do this you have to be exceptionally wealthy.

In Accra I stayed in the town household of a Kwahu family, their home residence being between Accra and Kumasi, in the depths of the countryside. In his country home the family head was a chief— *Kwame*, or "He who was born on Saturday." In his Accra house the chief became Harold, a prosperous merchant and a politician. His town house was large and rambling, on two floors. He occupied the upper floor with his wife by Christian marriage and their small children. It was a magnificent apartment, with every possible luxury—including a well stocked cocktail cabinet, for the one tradition that dies the hardest is the tradition of hospitality. In this apartment lived a happy, settled, thoroughly westernized family. But downstairs lived his other family, the family of Kwame as opposed to that of Harold—all his nephews and other appendages of his extended Kwahu family which, as Kwame, he felt obliged to support, even in Accra.

It was like going from one world to another, and I lived a completely double life with ease and pleasure in that household. Upstairs we drank whisky, danced the cha-cha and the mambo, ate bacon and eggs for breakfast and drank tea at tea time. From upstairs we sallied forth for evenings at the various smart night clubs (evening dress compulsory), or to elegant private dinner parties. But downstairs I ate *fufu** with my fingers, drank palm wine, danced *Abalabi*, and learned what real family life is like.

And downstairs I learned what the African man in the modern, civilized street feels like. As Harold, Kwame had made a pretty effective adjustment, and was able to live happily in Accra; as Kwame, he could live in Kwahu, without the one identity interfering with the other. But both Harold and Kwame, as separate personalities, had money in their own right: the one from business, the other from family inheritance. Downstairs the relatives did not

---

* *A kind of unsweetened dough made from manioc flour, from which one tears pieces to dip in a sauce.*

have money and were not able to commute, so to speak, from one way of life to the other. There was Kwabena, the undisputed head of the downstairs family. He was Harold's right-hand man in the commercial enterprise, and was also his heir in Kwahu, being his oldest nephew. But he was kept pretty much on a shoestring and had not been able to get much of an education. He depended on both worlds for his material as well as for his spiritual well-being, but he could not reconcile them. Had he just been a traditional heir he would have been content to live on in Kwahu until he succeeded to position and wealth. But as a member of the family of Harold, rather than of Kwame, he was violently dissatisfied. If he had had more money he might have been able to take a step further into the world he called civilized; he could have owned a house of his own, and a car, and he could have afforded a cocktail cabinet and elegant parties and dinners, and he could have been seen at expensive night clubs. If he had had less money, and less opportunity, he would probably have been content to stay at Kwahu as a hereditary landowner and junior head of a large extended family, with all the attendant responsibilities and privileges. As it was he fell between the two worlds and was at ease in neither. He was violently jealous of his uncle upstairs, and bitterly resentful of having to live downstairs "like a savage." Yet at the same time he was most critical of Harold's failures in his other role as Kwame.

He was particularly jealous of two teen-age nephews of Harold, who although they were also living downstairs, were obviously being very carefully schooled for subsequent launching into the upstairs world. It seemed that Harold regarded Kwabena, his senior nephew, as being his legitimate traditional heir, but as being unsuitable to take over his business. If the opportunity had come earlier, no doubt Harold would have given Kwabena a good education, but now it was too late, so he was training his two younger nephews, sending them to Achimota College, and later to the university. His own children, who under traditional law would have been brought up by their uncle, he trained similarly, but he obviously felt they were of less concern than his nephews.

And finally there was Kofi, a youth of about eighteen years and with a good high school education. He was a more distant relative, and Harold supported him only under protest, and he certainly had no expectations. He had come from Kwahu a year earlier, hoping to find a niche in the brave new world. He admitted he enjoyed the high life of the city, but he was deeply offended by the petty jealousies of the divided household. There was a conflict between belief and practice that he could not resolve, and that remained unresolved all around him, wherever he looked. And he never thought in terms of compromise—for him it was a question of abandoning one way or the other. He finally left the city and went back to Kwahu to work on a plantation.

All these people had a problem in adjusting to the impact of the two worlds, but it was not a problem colored, as it is in East, Central and South Africa, by racial animosity. Toward the Europeans they felt political hostility, but in general it was nothing more personal than that. And once they achieved a measure of political independence their feelings became even less personal. In this way, though a people such as the Ashanti had a vast and impressive history of great civilization behind them they were able to abandon it with relative ease for the western way, with its obvious political, economic and social advantages.

Elsewhere in Africa, where racial hatred has crept into both worlds, the entire world of the white man, as well as the white man himself, is hated, and the western way is adopted only with reluctance, and often with contempt, as a regrettable necessity. But in West Africa it is apparently adopted with exuberant enthusiasm and, at first sight, almost complete success. The lack of racial animosity has made such adoption possible without the implied connotation of treachery. So long as the West African maintained his political hostility he felt free to adopt the white man's ways as nearly completely as he could. But in so doing he convinced himself that he had no need of the past, that he was, in fact, westernized. It is only now, perhaps, after several years of increasing independence that he is beginning to realize that he has left something of real worth behind. The problem now is whether or not he can recapture that elusive something, or whether he has condemned himself, as a westerner, to materialism.

Kofi realized this, and made the choice of returning to Kwahu, where he knew he could possess something more than clothes and cocktail cabinets. Kwabena knew this when he criticized his uncle on the one hand for not devoting himself entirely to his duties as Chief Kwame, and on the other for not giving him more opportunity in the world of bright Accra lights and night clubs. And Harold knew it as he played his delicate game of balancing his various family relations and duties in his two worlds. The only thing that made it possible for him to succeed was his wealth. And he knew as well as any that his solution was by no means perfect—it was only another form of segregation.

It would be impossible to generalize on the overall feelings of urban Africans to the changing world they live in, but there is a common theme apparent in their attitudes and in their actions, every one of them. The theme is a sense of a lack of something in their lives. The new world they have embraced, with various feelings, leaves them with an emptiness, a void that they all recognize and all want to fill. On the one hand they regard it as something they have lost, something that has gone with the past, perhaps irrevocably; on the other hand they think of it as something they have not yet achieved. But there it is, eating away at them, making them, in extreme cases, either bitter or frustrated, in less extreme cases just bewildered. They see all around them disintegration of the things that they still value. The extended family is an impossibility in urban society, with its increased cost of living and new standards; ideals of economic cooperation die with difficulty under the new competitive economy; political allegiance, once given to the chief as the representative of the ancestors, is given to the new political leaders, but not with the same conviction.

Are they to continue the attempt to adopt the new way of life, or are they to pause now and try to understand what they are losing in the process? There are some who feel they are losing nothing; others feel that they are merely losing their self-respect in this wholehearted denial of the past. But there are many who see very clearly that they are losing the things they need to give life a meaning beyond the narrow meaning of nationalism or westernization, and yet can see no room for traditional life in the unbelieving world into which they have been born. For many of them Christianity is, at best, a very temporary and very local anesthetic. There is a desperate need for something that will fill the void, rather than just help them forget it exists.

2

Masoudi

Masoudi was a good-looking boy. He was bright and cheerful and willing to learn the ways of the *muzungu*, or white man. In those days white men were few and far between in the forest area, though Kisanganyi was rapidly growing into a great town called Stanleyville. But the white men had established a post at Matadi, some three days' walk from Masoudi's own village of Ndola. The name "Matadi" was taken from another village many months away to the west, or so Masoudi was told: he had never heard of it before.

And it was because he was good-looking as well as cheerful and bright, so the same accounts went, that Masoudi was asked by the Bwana Mkubwa, the administrator, to become his houseboy at Matadi. The villagers were used to such things from the Arab slave traders, so they were not unduly surprised that the white man should have the same strange and, to them, rather ludicrous customs. They did not expect it to last long, and soon Masoudi would be back among them.

Masoudi himself was reticent about those days; he merely said that the Bwana Mkubwa had been good to him for a time, but eventually sent him away—just about the age when he was gangling and awkward and feeling that he really should be showing some interest in the local girls. But the administrator was kind, and sent Masoudi to the one and only local Mission School.

At this school Masoudi was taught by the priest, before anything else, that he was evil; that he had committed the most un-forgivable of crimes, even for a savage. He recalled how funny it had seemed to him that the white men should call *him* a savage, when they were so plainly savages themselves. But anyway, he was taught that if he wanted to live forever (this also struck him as being funny) he would have to say he was sorry for being evil, and that from now onwards he would trust and obey the greatest white man of all, someone who was evidently even greater than the King of the Belgians: Bwana Yesu.

So, following the line of least resistance, and not really under-standing one bit of it, Masoudi became a Christian. There were certain annoying things about it, one of which was that when he tried to prove that he was not really like the animals and savages and white men, and that he knew how to behave toward girls, he was told he must not even do that, for it also was evil. He worked well, however, and learned how to read and write. During the holidays he worked in the administrative office at Matadi and became quite an efficient clerk. He would have liked to have learned French so that he could read some of the newspapers and reports he handled, but he was told it would not be good for him and all he managed was to pick up an odd word here and there.

The Mission eventually gave him up as one of their many failures, because Masoudi said he could not see why he had to refrain from doing so many perfectly natural things such as sleep-ing with the girls, smoking hemp, drinking home-brewed liquor and gambling. So he went ahead and did those things. Nor could he understand the administrator who had originally befriended him and who still took an interest in his career. The Bwana Mkubwa greeted him very coldly, if at all, and avoided him com-pletely after the day when Masoudi broached the subject and asked him if it was because of the girls, and did the Bwana

Mkubwa want him to sleep with him again? Shortly afterward Masoudi was sent back to his village.

He was just as glad, because he certainly did not want to sleep with the administrator, who had become excessively fat, and whose flesh was like that of the fat white slug, but he was puzzled. The white man had come and put an end to the fighting between the various tribes and that was obviously a good thing. He had not interfered with the ways the villagers lived their lives, other than by getting them to move all their villages down to the edge of the great road that was being built through the forest from Stanley-ville. This also was a good thing; the villages had to be moved every three years or so anyway, when the soil became exhausted, and there were great advantages to being near the road. It made intervillage markets easier and safer, and much more exciting. It meant that you could get from one village to the other without having to worry about wild animals or the dangerous forest spirits that preyed on villagers, killing and eating them.

The white man was obviously much more clever than the village people were, and had much more powerful magic. Why, then, with all this, did the administrator seem almost afraid of him; and why, if he did *not* like him, was he so kind and helpful in sending him to the Mission School and in teaching him how to be a clerk? And if he *did* like him why was he offended when Masoudi offered to give up girls and sleep with him again, which was what he had originally wanted?

The Mission puzzled Masoudi too, because they would never explain anything. When he asked at the office of the administration why he had to do something, it was explained to him. But at the mission, when he asked why he could not sleep with girls they simply said that it was bad, and that Bwana Yesu had said it was bad. Then when he inquired how, if Bwana Yesu had never slept with girls, could they all be his children, they told him he was evil. Masoudi tried hard to understand, because he liked the white man's ways; he liked the brick houses that did not fall down, he liked the funny way they stored water so that you did not have to go down to the river but just turned a thing called a tap; he liked the way they never went short of food but never bothered to grow any; and he was fascinated by the clothes, with pockets in the trousers and pockets in the shirts and pockets in the coats. Even on the hottest days he wore as many clothes as he could, though he could never find enough suitable objects with which to fill his pockets. That was another thing that puzzled him—*what* did the white man put in all those pockets? Even when I knew Masoudi, many years later, he was still obsessed by this problem. His prize possession was a white tunic jacket with four pockets outside and two inside, and in each one he had something—mainly a variety of different colored pencils, showing prominently to indicate that he could write; bits of string to show that he had important packages to tie up and send off by the *courrier;* scraps of paper and miscellaneous cigarette ends.

Back at Ndola, Masoudi found things difficult. He had been away for several years (he was hazy about the exact length of time, but it must have been six or seven years) although he had been back on a number of occasions for short visits. But then he had always been so full of tales of the white man, of the rapidly growing town of Matadi (in fact it was only a village), and of the extraordinary Mission, that he was always the center of attraction. The thing that he noticed about his relatives and friends was their interest in him and in what he had to say; what he did not notice was a certain change in their attitude, though on looking back he was sure that the change had begun, even then.

When he returned permanently, however, he found a change right away. For one thing, the village, like all others, was firmly established on the roadside. He did not think it unreasonable to build his house on the other side of the road, where there was more space; nor did he think anything of building it in the manner of the houses at Matadi, with several rooms, plenty of windows, and two heavy wooden doors that could be secured by the padlocks he had proudly brought back with him. The villagers, especially his relatives, however, accused him of being in league with the evil spirits, saying he was so unafraid of them that only he would risk having windows through which the spirits could enter, or through which they could stare with the Evil Eye. Or else he was so evil that he had windows on all sides so that he could spy on everyone and bewitch them with *his* Evil Eye. And why lock doors against friends and relatives? And why build his house apart from them?

But in his years away Masoudi had not only become an object of suspicion, he had also become an object of scorn. He was told that he was no better than the BaNgwana, who gave their boys to pleasure the Arab slave traders, and who eventually took healthy boys from the local tribes and made them into fools and simpletons in the same way. Perhaps *scorn* is too strong a word. Masoudi was laughed at, more than anything, for his relationship with the administrator, but when he tried to explain that it was the white man's custom, and the white man was obviously powerful and therefore the custom must be good, then the laughter of the villagers turned to suspicion. His explanation about the windows, his protestations that there were no such things as evil spirits and Evil Eyes, did not help, because everyone knew that there *were* such things.

When Masoudi looked for a wife he found out just how deep the suspicion went. He had inherited some wealth from his father, and had amassed considerably more while working in Matadi, so he had more than enough to pay a respectable wealth of goats and cloth and metal to any father willing to offer his daughter. But everyone wanted to know where all the goats had come from, how he had managed to get the cloth, when by his own admission he had not worked his own plantation in Matadi and so had not had any goods to exchange for these things. The notion of money and of working for wages was still foreign to the villagers in those days, and it was just another cause for mistrust which Masoudi could not explain away.

Eventually a girl was found whose father was willing to accept Masoudi as a son-in-law. She was, of course, from the same tribe, but of quite a different branch, and one into which his people did not generally marry. Their villages were just the other side of Matadi, and so they understood Masoudi better. When, according to custom, Masoudi brought his bride back to Ndola he was hurt to find that he was treated as more of a foreigner than ever.

But Masoudi had other things to think of. He now had a wife to help him with the plantation, and he began to cut down more forest so that he could grow more plantains and support a larger family. He wanted to have children that he could send to the Mission School to learn to read and write. He never worried about the peculiar way the missionaries thought, because it was so very peculiar that his children, no more than he nor any other sensible person, would ever take notice of it. But to read and write was obviously good. They could all work in Matadi and make lots of money.

It was not long after Masoudi's marriage that Ndola received a visit from the administrator himself. He asked the chief, Matungi, to call the village together. When everyone had assembled the Bwana Mkubwa told them that from now onwards they must all plant certain crops in addition to those they normally planted. Cotton was the chief innovation. He explained that when the cotton was picked the government would send around trucks to pick it up, and that everyone would be given pieces of metal and paper that could be exchanged for cloth and beads and all manner of other things at Matadi. In time there would even be a store right there in Ndola, where they could use this new money.

The administrator explained that this was necessary to make the work of the government possible, in setting up a hospital, dispensaries and schools. He also said that he wanted some of the men of Ndola to volunteer their services for work on the roads. He added that those who did not produce cotton, as required, would be locked up or compulsorily put to work with the road gangs; and that if there were not enough road-work volunteers they would simply be forced into service.

Matungi listened to all this courteously, and then asked for time to consult with the elders. The consultation evidently did not take long, and he returned to face the administrator and tell him that he was sorry, but his village wanted nothing to do with cotton or road work; they preferred simply to live as they had always lived, without this new money and the trade goods that it could buy.

The administrator, unwilling to use force so early in the program, argued his point and appealed to Masoudi, who, as usual, was standing apart from the others. Masoudi said that he had tried to tell his relatives about the ways of the white man, and about all the good things that were being done at Matadi, but they had not listened. He then harangued the village, not so much venting his own grievances, but trying to explain once again that although the ways of the white man were different from theirs, there was no reason why the two people should not get along as friends, each learning from the other and each benefiting from the other. The villagers listened with more respect than usual, but Matungi shook his head. He was adamant. The administrator could try elsewhere, find other villages for his cotton and other villagers for his road gangs. Ndola was not going to be polluted.

The administrator left, and nothing much happened for some months. Presumably he was sounding out other villages in the district. But eventually, backed up where necessary by the authority of armed native police imported from the north, all the recalcitrant chiefs and headmen were deposed, and more amenable successors

appointed. Masoudi was appointed Capita, or headman, in Matungi's place. Matungi made no objection, because he knew that
it would make little difference one way or the other, and he was
too sensible to argue with savages armed with guns. The government, with these armed savages, an animal people from the north
who did not even circumcise, would get their cotton and road
workers, but they would never break the sacred tie between him
and his people.

Masoudi felt much the same way. He knew that the people
would not give him the allegiance that was Matungi's, but that he
would have authority over them in other matters, in support of
which he could demand the assistance of the police. He recognized
that Matungi's position as ritual leader of the people would remain
unaltered. But this was his, Masoudi's, chance to prove to the
villagers that he had been right from the start; that he did not
possess the Evil Eye, that the ways of the white man were good, if
strange, that all of them could own many goats and metal pots
and pans, oil lanterns to see by night and a bicycle to ride from
one village to the next along the new road in a quarter of the time
it took to walk. He was convinced that he was right, that odd
though they might seem the white men certainly were powerful,
and the thing to do was to acquire the same power by copying
their ways. He even saw his friends and relatives eventually coming around to liking him again, and speaking to him and his wife.

At this time Masoudi was still clear in his mind that this course
of action was perfectly possible. As he saw it, Matungi was too
ignorant and superstitious to trust the white man and would never
give the white man a chance to show the worth of what he had to
offer. Matungi could neither read nor write, and had no desire to
learn. He was content to take a day to walk to the next village
instead of being able to go there and back, on a bicycle, in half
the time. Masoudi still had far too much respect for his own traditions and beliefs, particularly after seeing how ridiculous some

of those of the white man were, to expect Matungi's position to change overnight merely because the Bwana Mkubwa had given him the title that was rightfully Matungi's. But he accepted the responsibility, with pride and hope, intending merely to look after the cotton fields, to make sure that everyone planted the amount he was meant to plant; and he would see to it that there were enough volunteers for the road gangs. Matungi would continue to be chief in all but name in matters of tradition.

Masoudi admitted that he felt some gratification in having behind him the power of the police, though he had been refused a policeman of his own, such as the big chiefs had. If he had to use force to show his relatives that he was right about the white man he would do it. They deserved harsh treatment for the way they had behaved toward him. He saw himself as bringing them all multipocketed clothes, shining metal- and enamelware, oil lanterns and bicycles; in return for which all they had to do was to plant a little cotton and do a little work on the road.

Masoudi has long since given up that dream. He still holds to the conviction that many of the white man's ways of living are good, but he no longer believes that they can be transplanted. And he increasingly regrets having abandoned his heritage.

For Masoudi quickly found that he had both more and less authority than he had bargained for. He was efficient at seeing that the cotton was planted and harvested, for the administration sent people to help supervise until the villagers were accustomed to the procedure. He kept notebooks, listing everyone in the village, how much they planted and how much they harvested. He was prepared to take the blame for anyone who failed to produce the minimum amount, and he took such measures as he thought fit to prevent any failure. These measures included fines of chickens or goats, under threat of calling in the police to take the offenders away and put them in boxes. Of course he never intended to call the police. Masoudi was far too mild a man for that. So he was horrified when on one of his periodic visits a new young administrator ordered some villagers beaten for not having kept their plantations in good order. When he protested on their behalf, Masoudi was told that if he disapproved of beatings he had better keep a sharper eye on the work, and that if the plantations were as far behindhand on the next visit he would be beaten himself.

In fact the administration took all sorts of measures of which Masoudi disapproved strongly—such as compelling men to work on the roads and then fining them because they were behind with their work on the plantations. But in these matters he found that he had no authority at all. It was bitter that he should be blamed for these matters by the villagers, while at the same time he was blamed by the administration for other matters that, in Masoudi's eyes, fell under Matungi's jurisdiction. For instance, Ibrahimo's father complained to the administration that the villagers were trying to force his son to enter the initiation school, even though he had been named Ibrahimo after the father of Isaaka, and was therefore a Christian. Masoudi was promptly fined five chickens and told that he must stop Matungi from doing this kind of thing. Masoudi tried to explain that it was none of his concern, that Matungi was the acknowledged ritual leader, and the only one with ritual authority because he was born into it, but the administration merely fined him another five chickens and told him that he was capita and *everything* was his responsibility.

Masoudi had learned early the futility of questioning the why of the ways of the white man. He just accepted the fact that they did not understand him any more than he understood them, and he tried to make the best of his unhappy position. The government considered that he had taken over all Matungi's powers and responsibility, but from his point of view it was a sacrilege even to consider the possibility, and sheer stupidity to try to put it into practice. Yet if he was going to be fined every time Matungi did something wrong he would have to do something about it. And this was what worried him. The more he saw of the white man's ways, the more he fell back on his old beliefs, and to take any action against Matungi was in direct contradiction to all those beliefs.

It was not that Masoudi was any the less convinced about the desirability of many of the things the white man had to offer. Their clothes were far superior, even if, as he had been told, they were the real reason why his villagers had to plant that ridiculous cotton which everyone knew ruined the soil. The oil lanterns and bicycles were also good things, and so was the hospital in Matadi, and the traveling doctor who was much better at curing some illnesses than Matungi had ever been. Even the road was a good thing. But why did everyone have to get so upset over young Ibrahimo, who himself had wanted to enter the initiation school, just as every youngster should, but whose father had been bribed by Bwana Spence, of the Mission, to send him there to be circumcised? What Masoudi could never understand was why the white man expected him, and the others, to change their beliefs, to abandon the way of the ancestors. Why should it not be possible to continue in the way of the ancestors, the way they *had* to follow if they were not to be condemned to the world of spirits and ghosts after death, and still wear the white man's clothes, grow his cotton, and look after his roads? Did the black man expect the white man to change *his* beliefs, to abandon *his* traditions?

Yet Masoudi realized that whether he liked it or not his own beliefs had been changed, at least to some extent. He knew the villagers were wrong when they said he had the Evil Eye. They were merely resentful of his position and authority. He no longer believed in evil spirits and Matungi's magic, but he *did* believe in the ancestors. And so he was very unhappy when the administration told him that they expected him to discourage the initiation practices by which boys were made fit for afterlife and acceptable

to the ancestors. Without initiation they were no better than animals or uncircumcised savages such as the Zande police. He arrived at a rather unsatisfactory compromise whereby the period
of time allotted for the initiation was cut down from nearly a year
to only two or three months. He felt that he had done his best,
but on the one hand the administration accused him of not having
been strong enough, and on the other Matungi and the villagers
renewed their attacks on him as being possessed of the Evil Eye.

Whenever the village moved up or down the road in search of
fresh land to be ruined by the cotton, Masoudi always built his
house after he had seen where the others were building theirs. He
then set his apart, and only his immediate family would build
anywhere near him. The last time I saw him he had built his house
on a hillock overlooking the far end of the village. His house was
actually just behind the hillock, so that it could not be seen, but
his *baraza** was right on the crest and in its shade he would sit,
hour after hour, all alone. Down below, Matungi's *baraza* was
always filled with villagers, conducting village affairs as they had
always been conducted, without the slightest regard for their capita
up on the hillock. Matungi settled all the disputes without reference to Masoudi, and more and more the villagers came to accept
that Masoudi was not really evil, he just did not matter. They
began to talk again of his early association with the Bwana
Mkubwa in Matadi, and once again they laughed at him for an
empty-headed fool.

In time the villagers had come to submit without fuss to the
ever-increasing regulations about what crops they should or should
not plant, and they recognized that there were certain benefits
that went with this attitude. But they never accepted these benefits
as Masoudi did, as something that added to their lives or made

---

* *An open porch, used as a meeting place.*

them better or easier. They might have come to think differently
had it not been for Matungi, but he saw to it that there was no
weakening of their respect for the ancestors or for the ways of the
ancestors. In fact Matungi was so strong and so obviously right
in his attitude to the ancestors that Masoudi himself finally weak-
ened. Everything he had tried to do for the village had been
blocked by Matungi. Masoudi had finally managed to persuade
Bwana Spence, the missionary, to establish a small school at Ndola.
That way, he thought, the children would be able to learn to do
the same things that the white man did, though they would never
be stupid enough to share the same beliefs. But Matungi saw to it
that no children ever attended the school, apart from Ibrahimo, who
went there on the first day and was laughed at so that even his
father could not persuade him to go back. The rest of the children
simply left and went to visit the families of their mothers in
neighboring villages. Matungi even managed to persuade the villagers to refuse the medicine of the white man.

When Masoudi objected it was invariably when he was no
longer in control of his temper, and nothing could have been
worse. He had grown to be a singularly ugly little man, and he
dressed in a tunic far too big for him, wearing an old topee that
came down over his eyes. He was a ridiculous figure at any time,
but when he stamped on the ground in a fit of impotent rage in
front of Matungi, who continued to sit, as any chief should in front
of a commoner, in all the regality of his leopard-skin trimmings,
Masoudi lost any sympathy and respect that he might have had
from the villagers.

When talk of independence began to circulate, all that was
understood by the term was that the white man would leave. It
was then naturally assumed that Matungi would assume control
again; that cotton-growing and road-building would be abandoned,
and Masoudi forgotten. The villagers would have liked to
abandon the tiresome cotton right away, and the road work, but the

police were still there and kept them at it. The police, however, became more and more slack, wanting only to get back to their country in the north where men behaved decently and did *not* circumcise.

But the villagers could and did forget Masoudi. My last conversation with him, already old in his middle age, was in his *baraza* overlooking the village. I had known him over the course of some seven years and for the first time, perhaps, I saw what a change had taken place, even in that time. He seemed thinner and smaller as he huddled over his knees, clasping them as though he had to have something to hold onto. His eyes no longer held their old warm smile of welcome. Nor did they hold any bitterness or hostility. They were just horribly empty, as empty as the words he spoke. He had always looked on me as a renegade because I had failed to support him against Matungi. But even so, I was a white man, and I wore coats and shirts and trousers with innumerable pockets, so I still stood for something that he had wanted to be; something he felt that not only he but *all* his people should have tried to be.

But now he saw nothing in me; I suppose I was as much a shell to him as he was to me. I took my leave in the same way that I had taken it on two previous occasions in the past years, saying as usual that I would be back again soon. But he said no, this was the last parting. Looking down on the village that was his in name, but in which not even the children would speak to him, he said, "It is time for me to die. The village is Matungi's, the people are his. I am a stranger, and I have nowhere else to go."

Masoudi talked more than he had ever talked before, as though making a last effort to reassure himself of something. I tried to point out that when the Belgians left there would be a great need for every man who could read and write, and there would be plenty of responsible work for him to do in the government offices at Stanleyville or Matadi. He looked at me with his damp, empty eyes and said, "I died the day I left this village and went to Matadi—there is no point going back there. I am an old man [he could not have been more than in his late thirties] and I have only one worry. I believed in your world at one time, even if I did not understand it, and I tried to follow your ways. But in doing this I lost my spirit. It left me somewhere; perhaps in Matadi, perhaps when I interfered with the initiation. But somewhere it left me, and I am empty."

I was startled at his having put into words so exactly what my thoughts had been in looking at him and listening.

"In your world you people made me change to your ways, and tried to make me think like you. But no matter how hard I tried you never took me as one of yourselves. To you I was still a savage, and you used me for your own ends. I was content, because I knew that I could never be completely like you, but I thought that my children could learn, and their children would surely be just like you. I tried to bring help to my people by telling them of your ways, and by being their capita. But look at them, they do not even pay me the respect due to an old man: to my own people, as to you, I am just a savage. I am alone in this world. You made it impossible for me to be true to the ways of my ancestors, yet I can not understand the ways of your Bwana Yesu, I can not believe his beliefs. When I die, very soon, shall I still be alone? Will you talk to me then? Will my people talk to me? Will anyone speed my spirit on its way to some resting place, or shall I be as I am now, alone?"

Masoudi turned to look at me, fully and clearly. "It is you people who have made me like this . . ." but he stopped whatever it was he was going to say. He could not understand, so how could he ever hope to explain—even to himself. He summoned up a smile, though it seemed to take all his strength and will. He took my hand, clasping it in the old tribal form of handshake, and said quietly: "Go in peace, go well."

3

Something Old

If the spirit of western civilization, or indeed western civilization itself, is having a hard time establishing itself and surviving in modern Africa, the spirit of the past tradition is having an equally hard time. Those Africans who have had a real opportunity for getting to know the western way of life for what it is, and who have voluntarily decided that this is best for them, can seldom completely shake off the past—it is always there, influencing them in diverse ways, preventing them from becoming wholly western. But those who, either because they have not known it, or because they have lived more closely according to the traditional way, have tried to cling to the past have not been able to succeed either.

The time has gone when the extremists were dominant, those who wanted completely to abandon the one way for the other, though a few still persist. But the African of today is still caught in the same basic dilemma. Even in the city, where circumstances militate against traditionalism, there are those who adopt the outer forms of western civilization only where absolutely necessary and even then with reluctance. These are people who have either a conscious or an unconscious belief that the traditional way of life was at least as good as, if not better than, that of the West. They point to the disintegration of the family and dissolution of family ties and responsibilities, which, by extension of the concept of the family (a fundamental process of thought in traditional African societies), implies a breakdown of wider bonds linking the individual to the family at large, i.e., the clan, the tribe, and now the "nation." The traditionalists also point to a lack of any effective system of values, and the consequent moral instability. It can hardly be called immorality, they say, because there no longer are any morals, there is only law. This law, as they see it, is observed only for fear of the physical force that backs it, fear of physical punishment. They point to modern economics and modern politics as being founded on expediency rather than principle. In all these aspects of life they find that the traditional way was sounder because there was an overall unity achieved by a respect for a far greater power than that of the modern police force with its jails, firing squads or execution chambers. For these measures can only affect our life here, whereas the power that underlay the old society was based on man's concern for his ultimate afterlife existence, a concern that outweighed by far man's concern for his current, temporal existence.

Such traditionalists can be found in every modern city in Africa. They are, of course, thinking in tribal terms rather than national, and others point out that the concept of the family, which could be extended until it included an entire tribe, all members of which were theoretically related through some probably mythical ancestor, can hardly be extended to include a nation comprised of many different tribes, all with different ancestors. Also, nontraditionalists point out, the whole nature of the economy is changing; and the family in traditional Africa was essentially an economic unit.

The traditionalists acknowledge this, but they ask which is the more important—the traditional concept of the family, and all that it stands for, or modern economic and political theory. Why, they ask, should priority be given to the latter, and well proven values be expected to change to suit? Why should not priority be given to traditional values, many of which are demonstrably lacking in western society, and the economic and political systems be adapted to them? But by and large these traditionalists do not have any voice in the government; they are mainly private individuals who live according to their lights, accepting as inevitable that they are in a minority and will ultimately die out completely. And they are sad, because when they say that their old ways had many things to offer that western civilization has lost, they know with bitter certainty that they are right, and they know that these are the things that have made life worth living, and living well. There is, for the traditionalist, a spark of brightness, a purpose and meaning in the old way that does not exist in the new. And it is difficult not to agree with him when you look at some of the more blatant attempts at westernization.

There are those who try to preserve that spark. Sometimes they appear, on the surface, to be the most sophisticated and westernized. There was a priest who poured the Communion wine on the ground as a libation to the ancestors because he believed that this was more meaningful not only to himself, but to his parishioners. It was no sacrilege in his eyes, he said, he was merely translating the ritual language. But beneath this explanation, given with tongue in cheek, there was a deeper meaning, a wider understanding. I was told "The church may have lost faith in me—but I have not lost faith in Christianity."

This man, by virtue of his calling, might have been considered westernized. But his concept of the religion he had adopted was different from that of his teachers; it was broader, and perhaps deeper. To him the form of the ritual was relatively insignificant, it was the fact of Communion that was important. It would be difficult to say whether he thought that his parishioners would grasp the fact more readily through the usage of the familiar pagan ritual, or whether he himself felt that the pagan ritual was at least as valid as that of the Christians, and perhaps more so. As I understood him, it was a different way of looking at the old beliefs, and the old beliefs still stood firm in his mind. And they stood firm, not in opposition to Christian belief, but as part of it; as right and good. Christianity as so many of us understand it was, for him, too narrow and exclusive. If there was truly only one God, then obviously we must all have been worshiping the same God by different names. The only significant change that I could see between his new belief and his old was that whereas he once had believed that the gods of the neighboring tribes were powerful entities hostile to his own, he now believed that in fact they were all one and the same. And this made him much more "Christian" than many of the more orthodox followers of that religion who would have accused him of sacrilege for using Communion wine as a libation, but who found no difficulty in hating and even killing their fellow Christians. For this renegade suddenly found a once hostile world open to him in terms of friendship, trust and love. To say the least, the attitude of the orthodox confused him.

There was another priest in Ghana, who showed me with great pride a shrine his parishioners had built with their own hands, carving the steps of Calvary out of a mountainside, leading past grottos filled with locally carved figures to the shrine on the summit, with a magnificent Christ crucified carved by a Muslim from the north. Father Tawia had seen nothing wrong in accepting the labor of pagans for his all-African enterprise, and he was particularly delighted that a Muslim should have volunteered to carve and contribute the huge crucifix. But his white brethren held up their hands in horror and did everything possible to prevent the shrine from being completed. Their intolerance was such that one Easter Day, unfittingly enough, I witnessed a riot in the cathedral because they refused to allow Father Tawia to give Communion to the white congregation. Needless to say they blamed the whole thing on Father Tawia, who for some hours had been sitting with me talking about how he was struggling hard to believe in the church as deeply as he believed in Christianity.

Both these African priests, and many African converts whom I

talked with and came to know, had the same difficulty of reconciling the church with Christianity. Partly because they saw in Christianity another way of expressing their own traditional beliefs, or
of enlarging them and making them more appropriate to the
changing situation. But it was also partly because they saw in the
church an intolerance and narrowness that was even greater than
that of their pagan beliefs; and in the light of the Christian teaching of brotherhood, therefore, they felt their pagan community
to be more Christian than the church.

If the logic does not appeal to us, we should remember that
we are constantly judging the African from *our* point of view,
which is an act that itself is logical only if we admit our bigotry,
or insist on our absolute superiority (either equally insulting to the
African). We should not object if the African judges us by our
own professed standards and finds that his traditional ways and
beliefs are more in accordance with those standards than are ours,
and more consistent with practice. If we were to make the effort
to understand that traditional ways and beliefs are by no means
always inferior to ours, nor even so very different once we see
below the surface, we could sympathize with the thoroughgoing
traditionalist instead of merely judging him. He can see and
understand the good in his own way of life, and feels safer in
holding onto it than he does in leaving it in favor of something
that is in basic values not so demonstrably superior, and in actuality is so extraordinarily confusing, full of self-evident contradic-
tions and apparent hypocrisies.

The traditionalists you find in urban centers are unlike those in
tribal areas. The urban traditionalist has seen our way of life and
has consciously rejected it, out of a far greater understanding than
the tribal African could have with his much more tenuous contact
with white civilization. He has made the comparison and formed
his judgment, often in remarkably cold, sober, unemotional ra-
tionality. Yet in many ways he is much less fortunate than his

tribal fellow, for the urban way of life militates in so many ways against fully traditional behavior. Not only is it impractical to have many wives, a custom that is occasionally ordained by tradition, and not only is it economically almost impossible to support an extended family in an urban context, even at the lowest level of sophistication, and not only is it obviously politically impossible to retain traditional authority in competition with, or at least in coexistence with the urban authority of a nontraditional governmental system; but there are subtler factors that prevent effective traditionalism in urban communities.

These factors are similar to the typical European imports of social snobbery and exclusiveness, but they act with all the force of traditional sanctions of ridicule and exile. In traditional society, widespread throughout Africa, ridicule and the threat of exile are as effective in the maintenance of law and order and of conformity of behavior as are the ghastly forms of physical punishment that we have often grossly exaggerated and held to be the sole basis of tribal authority in Africa. So the possibility of being laughed at for having two wives, or for respecting the ancestors, and the threat of being debarred membership from the various clubs for refusal to wear appropriate western dress, are all the more powerful because of the traditional nature of their threat. And by the same token these threats of ridicule and exclusion for being a traditionalist result in an unknown but undoubtedly significant proportion of alleged nontraditionalists, and often underlie the vehemence of the professed antitraditionalists.

Another reason for the difficulty traditionalism has in urban society is that western teachings, particularly those of the missionaries, have often at least induced skepticism where they have not made converts, and in the absence of thoroughgoing belief traditionalism dies a sure death.

Even to profess respect for tradition in contemporary urban African society you have to be relatively wealthy. There are many who compromise by having both a town and country residence, and I know a man who takes part in the government of his country in the coastal capital, where he lives in a modern house with his Christian wife and his children, as a law-abiding citizen, yet who maintains three other wives in his country home, where his primary responsibilities are not to his sons so much as to his nephews. In this way he may not seem to be so different from Harold, alias Kwame. But his traditionalism in the country goes even further, since although he is not even a magistrate, the local police prefer to send him cases to be judged because in their eyes he is still the chief, and all that goes with that position. He judges the cases with a mixed respect for both traditional and contemporary law, and as far as I know there have never been any complaints made by those brought before him and judged by him.

He wears traditional clothes in the country, and holds the traditional symbols of his office, representing his divine as well as his secular authority. He feels bound by the traditional moral code, which imposes heavy obligations and responsibilities on a chief, and he performs the necessary rituals demanded by his position. His three wives and large extended family household are vitally important, both to him and to the people whose chief he is, as symbols not only of his wealth and status, but of the fact that he has been blessed by the gods. Without them he would be a nonentity.

I suspect that his Christian wife and small individual family in the city are equally regarded by him—and others—as symbols of status. Like many others he retains, even in the city, certain traditional ways. He wears western clothes during the daytime, but in the privacy of his home, in the evening, he wears his customary robes. He looks down on those who wear their robes ostentatiously in public as hypocrites or exhibitionists. And, also like many others, when there is some occasion such as the christening of a child, he not only has a ceremony performed in church, but he makes doubly sure, even in the city, by pouring a libation of gin on the ground. I have even seen this done in England, at a chic christening party for the first son of another important West African chief. There the gin was poured, without concern, over a valuable Persian carpet. It was done neither as a gesture of bravado, nor in complete sincerity, but in a loneliness of mind that wanted desperately to believe, but that did not know what to believe.

In discussing this ambicultural nature with extreme frankness, the chief-cum-politician was very definite about which way of life he preferred and respected more. Perhaps it was partly because we were at that time in his country home and he was being his chiefly self, but even in the city he spoke in much the same vein. He said that he had no doubt at all that his own traditional values were not only the more important to him, but also the more valid, even in his urban life. But it was practically impossible to uphold them in urban society, even had he been wealthy enough, and so he was forced into this double life. It was impossible, he found, to be a thoroughgoing traditionalist in the city, but although he therefore adopted the trappings of western culture his beliefs remained unchanged.

"I take the superficialities of your civilization for what they are worth," he said, "and they are convenient modes of behavior, that is all. When I am thinking as a politician it is still the way of my ancestors that governs my thought and my judgment, because these are the only things I believe in. I know that when I am away my Christian wife sleeps with other men, for that is the way of the city. But I also know that she sends the children to her brother's home, and that is good—it follows our custom."

I asked him why, if his beliefs were still traditional, he had married this wife in the church. He answered, "It was convenient, and in the city it was expected. That wife is my youngest wife, and so all the other wives think of her as getting special treatment, which is also expected. That is why she so seldom comes to the country, because the others are her seniors, and because of her immorality she is not respected."

He went on to say that he took part in politics because he felt that someone with a respect for tradition should be in the government. Otherwise, he said, he would have nothing to do with the city. His greatest argument against it, and against the western way of life that went with it, was that it involved the destruction of the family, and the family is the center of traditional life almost throughout Africa. And with the destruction of the family comes the destruction of morality, because to this man, as to many Africans, not to do something merely for fear of the force of secular law and of physical punishment is not being moral, it is merely being prudent. True morality, for the African, springs from the relationship of a human being to his family, for the family can be traced back to a common ancestor from which all the tribe are descended, and it is therefore family considerations that determine his relationship with every other member of the tribe. And even more than this, the family consists not only of the living, or even of the dead, but also the unborn. At this highest extension of the family the African is brought directly into contact with the supernatural, with his ancestors, with the Divinity, the unknown. But here again morality is saved from becoming a mere conformity based on fear, albeit of the supernatural, because it is respect rather than fear that is the dominant characteristic of family life; and respect, at least to some extent, is voluntary.

Traditionalists have a hard time in urban areas also because these are the areas where Europeans have for the longest time been consistently teaching the Africans that all their traditional ways and beliefs are savage and evil. It is not surprising that many Africans have come to believe this themselves; particularly as the necessarily changed way of life in these urban communities has made traditionalism inoperable and therefore, in the course of time, incomprehensible. Tradition can be understood only in its entirety, and at the most there are only a few isolated customs, such as the pouring of libations, that remain in urban centers. Being isolated, they have no direct reference and relationship to life as a whole, and this increases the suspicion of the would-be-western African that tradition really is useless, if not savage.

Looking back on his own past the sophisticated African shares our horror at practices not so long dead—such as the mass executions on the death of the King of BaGanda, sometimes amounting to thousands of men, women, and children; the cannibalism of some of the Congo tribes; the savage punishments of the Ashanti, such as *atopere*—the dance of death where the victim is slowly sliced to death while being made to dance until, just before he dies, his head is sawn off. The African shares the general western opinion that the great kingdoms and empires of the past (the Kabaka of BaGanda can trace his ancestry back in an unbroken line a great deal further than, say, the British royal family) were founded on oppression and cruelty, and certainly there has been no lack of evidence of human sacrifice to support this view. But what is not so often mentioned is that these sacrifices generally took place during the interregnum between the death of one king and the accession of another. Properly understood they are no longer mere orgies of unnecessary and willful bloodshed, but they appear as essential, if drastic, measures to insure the maintenance of internal order.

Some of the great kingdoms and empires of Africa date back many hundreds of years. Ethiopia was a flourishing Christian kingdom with an elaborate court at a time when England was still overrun by petty clans of near-naked heathens. Sub-Saharan Africa can boast equal, if not greater, monarchies following at least from the thirteenth century onward. By the time Portuguese traders began to investigate the coastline in the sixteenth century, the Ashanti were in the process of consolidating one of the most powerful confederations ever known, and the Congo was divided into a number of equally powerful kingdoms and empires, each gradually assimilating neighboring tribes and "civilizing" them. East Africa had its kingdoms, and the rulers were criticized and judged by us as ruthless despots, violent and constantly at war, motivated only by greed and desire for personal wealth and power. This is what we have taught the Africans, and what many of them have come to believe. Yet the traditional ruler in Africa was by no means generally despotic. Most of the political systems were, in fact, remarkably democratic. The ruler's power was subject to innumerable checks and his own position was one of extreme insecurity. Security could only come from charisma—he had to deserve the position he held, and he had to continually demonstrate his fitness. Ruthless autocracy was simply impossible.

Unfortunately the opportunity for field work, which made the study of these societies possible and which has only recently begun to give us an insight into their real nature, came too late; opinion had already been formed. It is changing now, slowly, but oddly enough it is changing more rapidly in the western world than it is in Africa. As they achieve nationhood the Africans try to look to the past for something with which they can identify themselves, but they look to history, even to prehistory, rather than to the traditions that still live on in the rural areas in their midst.

Even in the rural areas skepticism has been introduced and a large number of people still live a tribal way of life but live it because it is the only way of life they know rather than because they believe in it.

The problem that the African people face is not so much whether to completely adopt the new or to attempt to recapture the old, since both aims are demonstrably impossible (with the inevitable rare individual exceptions). It is rather that in light of the fact that their way of life *has* been changed, and is going to change increasingly and inevitably, they are faced with the question of how to reconcile this with either a belief in the past, to which the traditionalists still cling, or the acceptance of a foreign belief which even the antitraditionalists acknowledge is usually superficial. The problem, at its most acute in the westernized city, results either in the abandonment of all belief, which is perhaps the most logical solution, or else in the adoption of the outer form of western belief without any inner conviction. This applies not only to religious belief, but also to political and economic and social life. And in each case it leaves either a terrible spiritual void and emptiness of purpose, or else the desperation of sheer materialism, both of which threaten to destroy the Africans as a people in their own right. It is only the traditionalist, leading his double life, or the alleged Christian, who interprets his own traditional beliefs through Christian rituals, who still retains some kind of moral or spiritual roots, and even they have to fight to survive on the impoverished soil around them. Even the Muslim Africans, whose faith is infinitely stronger than that of most Christian Africans, suffer from this conflict.

4

Matungi

Matungi is a man I have known well over a number of years, and this is his story as he told it to me, not on one occasion, but during the course of many long conversations. Matungi is a lover of tradition but he is also a shrewd and intelligent man, and he has seen the inevitable destruction of tradition creeping up on him for most of his life. So he is also a sad man. He is sad, not for himself, because he still believes with a strength that is compelling but gentle; he is sad for the young who have little belief, and for the unborn generations that will have none.

He is probably not much more than fifty years old, yet he is worn and exhausted. Despite the indignities he has suffered, he is still a proud man. Because he is great, he is unembittered. In everyday dealings, he is shrewd and calculating, and rather unscrupulous; but when it comes to matters of belief, he is a plain man who speaks and acts in strict accord with his principles, and he has nothing but contempt for those who do otherwise.

"You white people had not come to live here when I was a child, and your teachers did not set up their schools until they needed to make use of us. Then I was a man. So I was thought of, conceived and born in the manner of my ancestors, and I became a man in the manner of my ancestors. My mother had never eaten strange foods, nor been forced to do strange work, so her belly was clean and her milk was clean and I was clean.

My father was a good man. He was young when Bulamatadi (H. M. Stanley) came through our country three times, making war on everyone, but he fought back. He fought just as he fought the BaNgwana who stole our people and sold them to the Arabs, and just as he would have fought anyone who threatened his family. He was not like Effundi Mustafa, that old hypocrite who smiles in your face and poisons the food he offers you with evil thoughts. Effundi Mustafa says he sat on Bulamatadi's knee, and it is probably true, for he was a child then. But my father would have killed me before he would have allowed me to be so defiled. Because of these feelings, and because of all the fighting, he had to run away with many others to the country of the BaLese, and there, for want of BaBira girls, he married my mother. But this is not a bad thing for a chief's son to do. It helps to make friends with those who live around us . . . except with the BaNgwana. They do not know what friendship is, and their mouths lie even before they speak; we would never marry with them.

Not long after I finished drinking my mother's milk my father returned here. His own father had been killed by Bulamatadi. He had heard that the white men were all in a camp and were ill for shortage of food. He thought he would bring some bananas and make peace, for the camp was on the edge of his old plantation. But he and all the others with him were killed as they approached. It was like this wherever Bulamatadi went . . . he would have killed all of us, just as he killed his own men or left them to die. This is the man on whose knees Effundi Mustafa sat.

When the other white men came later we were afraid, because we thought that they too had come to kill us. For a long time they left us alone. They built their villages and we used to give them food. They called the chiefs together and said they came in friendship and wanted to help us, and particularly they wanted to stop us from fighting among ourselves. This was a good thing, because for too long we had been fighting. That was the fault of the

BaNgwana, because the BaNgwana used their magic to turn men's minds and make them traitors, so that they told where our camps were and how we could be surprised and captured. In those days we could trust nobody except our own family, and sometimes even they were bewitched.

I was chief in my father's place then, and even though I remembered what had happened to my father I offered to help the white man. They accepted my help, and for many months they ate my food. Then more and more white men came, and their villages grew. They brought some of their own food with them, yet they needed more of ours than we could spare. They did not do their own work but they asked us to supply men and women to do their work for them. I refused, because our people had work enough to do to keep their own fields cultivated and their own roofs thatched without working for foreigners. The white men said that in that case we would have to supply them with more food. They did not ask, they demanded, as though it was their land. I told them that it was my land, and my father's, and his father's before him, and that if they wanted to stay as my guests they were welcome to use the land to make their own plantations—there was room enough for all—but they would have to do their cutting and planting themselves. They said they had come to help us, but all they did was to send out men with guns whenever any of us reported any fighting among our neighbors. It was a good thing to stop the fighting, and we had all agreed. But when their men with guns started forcing us to work it was a bad thing. I took my family and my village and we all moved away deep into the forest and lived like savages until we could build another plantation.

The BaNgwana were the only people who helped the white man then, and they sold themselves just as they had sold us before. And it was the BaNgwana who told the white man exactly where we were living in the forest so even there we were not free from their guns. If we had had guns we would have driven them out, because they had not come to help us as they had said, they had come to make us slaves on our own land. But we had no guns.

After some years the white men were so many that they were able to send parties of soldiers into the forest. Their soldiers were not white, they were black like us, but they came from tribes to the north who were our enemies, so they were not on our side. We were forced to move back to where the white men were building the big road that now runs from Kisanganyi (Stanleyville). It took many years to build, and they demanded that we supply men— so many from each village—as well as food for all their soldiers, who stood with their guns in case we tried to escape. The white men did not always carry guns themselves, often they carried whips and they beat us like animals.

I remembered my father, and I said I would not let my people work for them. Because of the guns that had brought my people back to the roadside I said that we would supply whatever food we could spare, and for a time the white men accepted that. But they were not pleased. Then they came around and told us we had to plant cotton and other things we did not want to plant. They said they would pay us but I explained that if we planted cotton we would have to grow less food. They said we could buy food with the money we got for the cotton and I told them this was like the play of children, because we could easily grow our own food without money, and have enough left over to give them.

It was then that they told me that I was not a man, that I was evil, that I did not want to help my people, that I only wanted to make trouble. Therefore, they said, I was no longer chief. Masoudi was to be chief in my place. Masoudi was a weak young man who had been to one of the first schools set up by the white men, near their village of Matadi. He was like Effundi Mustafa. He had come from a BaBira family, but had followed the Ba-Ngwana and sold himself to the white man. He had no heart, had no spirit. He was as you see him now, an empty shell filled with the words and thoughts of foreigners. He was not one of us. I told the white men that Masoudi could never be chief, because of this reason. He was a Christian as well, and that meant he could not lead the people as the representative of their ancestors, and he could not initiate men into manhood. Nobody would follow him.

The white men simply said that the people might not follow him, but they would obey him because if they didn't the police would be sent in with their guns. In any case, they said, tribal initiation was thoroughly evil and a wasteful thing. Didn't we realize that all the time the boys were doing nothing in the initiation camp, for month after month, they could be working on the plantations or on the road gangs? I tried to explain that initiation was necessary for us, for only by initiation can we fit ourselves to join the ancestors when we die. The uninitiated have no right to respect in this life or after, and without initiation man would become an animal, living for himself alone, with no consideration for his family or his tribe.

I remember that was the first and last real argument I had with the white men. I tried hard to explain the way matters were with us, because I knew they were doing a terrible and wrong thing. But they would not listen. They were as children or as fools who can talk but can not reason, who can see but can not understand. Talk with such people is empty. Their heads were filled with strange notions. They said that we were to supply men to work alongside the BaNdaka, even with the Zande savages from the north . . . they only had enough sense to realize that nobody would work with the BaNgwana. They said we were all one people, even though we all speak different tongues. They said we were all friends, even though we are enemies. They said we were all under one God, by which they meant *their* God, and his son, the King Leopold. Here maybe they were right, for their God seems more powerful than ours, and more terrible and bloody. [It was here that Matungi paused to ask me questions that were difficult to answer. How could our God be a God of peace and love when his symbol is a heart torn out and shown mutilated with thorns and dripping with blood; when we like to remember him as a tortured figure savagely nailed on a cross; when he insisted on our magically eating his flesh and drinking his blood every week; and when he gave us guns? And how could he be a good God when he allowed his people to fight among each other and kill each other all the time? It was all very well to fight people of a different god, like the BaNgwana, or the Azande or even the BaNdaka, though they were closer, but for a people to fight among each other, among one's own kindred, and then boast about it, this was to Matungi as incomprehensible as it was evil.]

The chief of the white men came to our village himself and called all the people together. He told them that I was no longer chief, that Masoudi was. People were astounded, because to them this was a heresy, and they expected the white man to be struck dead. But I stepped forward and said that the white man's head was turned by the sun and he did not understand that Masoudi could never be chief. However, Masoudi was like white men, so let him call himself chief, and let him take on all the foolishness of trying to deal with them. I told my people that I wanted nothing to do with the white man, and I did not want to be responsible to the ancestors for polluting the soil of our fathers by following the white man's ways. I gladly gave up being a chief in the eyes of the white man, but to them, my people, I would remain as I had always been.

This pleased the village, and I think it even pleased Masoudi, who also knew that he could never really be chief. But the white men caught me and told one of their soldiers, an Azande, to beat me. For this I have never forgiven them. They could have beaten me themselves, for they had proved themselves stronger with their guns, and it would have been no disgrace. But to have me beaten by one of those savages from the north is a shame I shall never forget. Even our enemies we treat like men, not like children. For a long time this made me burn inside with a fire, eating at my stomach, eating my strength and my sense. But I became wiser, and now that I know the white man better I do not feel hot; because he will kill himself as surely as he kills others. In trying to destroy the pride of others he loses his own, and becomes a worm. Look at them now. They are truly a people who fight themselves. They pretend they fight us, but they eat out of their own hearts and their own souls, and they are empty flesh. When they are gone there will be nobody to weep, only rejoicing. They lie so much to others, they cheat and they steal from each other and they sleep with each others' wives. They may be more powerful than we but we are greater, because we are men, not animals.

After Masoudi became chief I had nothing to do with the white men for some time. I thought that if I left them alone they would leave me and my people alone, and for a while it was so. Masoudi saw to it that cotton was planted, and that there were extra plantains to feed the road gangs, and he told some men to work on the roads. They asked me if they should do these things, and I told them that these things were nothing to do with me—they were white men's matters and Masoudi was the white man's chief. If they did not obey, then the white man would simply send in his foreign soldiers with whips and guns and lock them up in cages, like animals.

Even then I did not realize just how evil the white man was. I thought he was merely stealing our land, and sometimes our lives. This is to be expected when one tribe is stronger than another and when it needs more room for its people. But they were not content with this—they wanted to steal our souls as well.

It is our custom to come to the head of the family whenever there is any dispute we can not settle, and if the head of the family can not deal with it, he takes it to the chief. If the chief can not settle it, he takes it to the paramount chief. We do this because we believe it is better for disputes to be settled as simply as possible, and by the people themselves. It would be easy for the chief to settle all disputes simply by commanding, but this would merely stop the fight, it would not cure the wound. So we discuss our grievances, and all members of the family take a part because blame is seldom on one side alone. In this way many disputes were brought to me because I was the senior member of our village, Masoudi was not. I come from the oldest branch of the family. Men who were having trouble with their wives would bring their cases to me; women whose husbands failed to give them children or who beat them too often also came. Complaints about the Ba-Ngwana and their bad magic always came straight to me, because I knew how to deal with those savages, for I have magic of my own.

But Masoudi did not like this, and he complained to the white man. The white man came and told me I was to hear no more cases, for I was no longer chief. Masoudi was to hear them, and record them in a special book, or send the disputants to the tribunal at Matadi if the case was serious. The white man said that if he ever heard that I was trying cases again, he would have me locked up in one of his boxes. He had been building these boxes at Matadi, and now he had a whole building full of them. Many men went in and never came out. There is a big graveyard right beside it, even today, and men are buried there without any consideration for the ancestors, and their souls are lost.

I paid little attention to the white man's warnings, because my people still would not go to Masoudi. I talked to Masoudi and told him that I would not interfere with his work, but that he was not to interfere with mine. If anyone brought a case to him he could enter it in his book and send it to the tribunal, but that he was not to let his eyes see what I was doing. He understood, and so I continued to be what I was, the real chief.

I had one other big fight with the white man though, and it was this fight that convinced me he was evil. Through Masoudi he managed to get all he wanted in the way of cotton, plantains and road workers. In time he came to collect taxes from all of us, out of the money he paid us for the cotton and plantains. The rest of the money he took back by fining us for various things, but none of this worried us very much. It was what we expected from a conquering people. But then the white man began to say that we were not to have more than one wife, and that we were to stop exchanging gifts of wealth at times of marriage. In this way he made many men and women lose their self-respect. What pride can a woman have if her husband does not think highly enough of her to give her parents a gift of many goats as a token of his esteem and trust? And what safety and happiness can the parents feel if they can not say, 'Our son-in-law has given us so many goats he must intend to treat our daughter well and to care for her, for no man could afford to lose so much wealth'?

But even worse than this, the white man began to try to prevent our holding our initiation ceremonies, celebrating the manhood of our youth. They said that if we wanted to educate the boys we should send them to a mission school where they would learn to recite from a book. They said that our initiation schools were savage, and a waste of time. For all those months the boys and their fathers were secluded they could not work in the fields, and so fell behind in their work demanded of them by law. And during all this time even the women fell off in their work because they were busy drinking and dancing. In addition the white man added their lie that these schools were for no other purpose than to stir up discontent. If it were not so, why did we not allow the white man in to watch and supervise?

I told the white man that we did not let him watch because he would defile our youth with his filth; that his eyes were evil, and he could only bring evil to our souls; that his body was unclean and he would desecrate the holy ground of the ancestors; that his mind was twisted and he would only see and tell untruths; that his heart was stone and he would not understand and respect and so he could only bring unhappiness to us and to our ancestors. If it were otherwise, as it was with you, we would let him see— provided he purified his body and mind and heart in the way we do. But it could not be otherwise with him, for white men are what they are, animals. I told him that neither I nor my people would ever fail in our duties to the ancestors, and initiation is the highest duty, for only by initiation can we fit ourselves to join the ancestors when we die.

He did not like my words, but he listened. He was angry, but he saw that I and my people would never give way. He told me that people like myself should be locked away in a box forever, that we were concerned only for ourselves, that we did not wish the good of our people. I walked away and left him talking to himself.

Every three years I called out the dancers and we held initiations in all the villages around us, for even though I am chief only of this village, I am the initiation leader of many villages. And every three years the white men went around trying to persuade mothers not to let their sons enter. But I told the mothers that this was because the white men did not want the children to become men, that they wanted them to live and die as children, unfit to join the ancestors, because in this way white men would gradually win all the land, and we would just die out, with a home neither in this life nor in the afterlife. And so the women always entered their children, and the children became men, and we still survive and we are still worthy of our ancestors, still worthy to live on the ground they won for us. And one day it will be ours again, completely.

Only once did I get into real trouble—and that was over a young boy whose father was a Christian, and who had sent the boy to a mission school. He was the only Christian of his kind in Ndola, though there were a number of others of different kinds in the same village. They never talked to each other and they had different ceremonies and different priests. They said bad things about each other all the time. The young boy, Ibrahimo, was much more friendly with his own people than he was with the Christians, unlike his father. He wanted to join his friends in the initiation, and become a man with them, because he knew that otherwise he would be alone, like his father, not belonging anywhere. Being a Christian did not seem to make him part of the white man's world, anyway. So I tried to persuade Ibrahimo to come with me, and I tried to persuade his father. His mother also tried to persuade her husband, but our efforts were empty. The boy was collected in a car and taken away, far to the other side of Matadi, to a mission hospital. There he was circumcised, and the white man said that was as good as our circumcision, so we should treat him like a man. But now Ibrahimo can never become a man—he has had manhood taken away from him by the white man, and he has had his soul taken away from him. Perhaps when he dies he will go to the white man's world, but that can not be a good thing; and as long as he lives here he will belong nowhere.

Because of all I did, and because of a curse I put on Ibrahimo's father to make him give way to his wife and child, I myself was sent to the tribunal at Matadi, and once again they threatened to put me in a box. But the ancestors were with me, and I was merely fined and told to go. I paid the fine with goats and chickens I stole from Masoudi, because it was really his doing, and I put a curse on Ibrahimo's father that people should always steal from him, just as he had stolen the very life from his son.

I have tried hard to understand the white man and his ways, but I can only see harm. What happiness have they brought us? They have given us a road we did not need, a road that brings more and more foreigners and enemies into our midst, causing trouble, making our women unclean, forcing us to a way of life that is not ours, planting crops we do not want, doing slave's work. At least the BaNgwana left us our beliefs, but the white man even wants to steal these from us. He sends us missions to destroy our belief and to teach our children to recite fine-sounding words; but they are words we believe in anyway, most of them. And we live according to our beliefs, which is more than the white man does. And the missions teach the children to have no respect for their parents. Is that a good thing? And they take them away from their parents, and then the other white men take them away to foreign lands. They say these lands are not foreign, because they are next to ours—but they must be foreign, because their beliefs are different. The circumcised can not live with the uncircumcised. Let the uncircumcised live by themselves, for them that is the right thing to do, and we have no quarrel with them for that—it is merely not our way. But let us live our way, because for us that is right.

The white man talks of law where we talk of the way of our ancestors; he talks of what is right or wrong where we talk of what is good or bad. I have looked at their way and do not like it, and I do not believe it is good for our people. It is better to do something because one believes in the ancestors than because one is afraid of being beaten or put in a box. And it is better to believe that something is good because goodness comes from it, than merely to say, "It is so because we have written it so in our book." Perhaps the white man believes in his own way; if so, let him keep it, and let us keep ours, and let us both be men, not animals.

In the initiation schools, we teach our boys about the ancestors that gave them birth, and they are born again by the ancestors, as men. We teach them how they must behave as men in order to live in a way pleasing to the ancestors, so that when they die they will live in peace. And that is why they find it easy to live the way they should—no man wants to die to be left alone, unwanted in either world, as Ibrahimo will die.

The white man says we teach our children to hate the white man in our initiation schools. We do not. We merely teach them to believe, and to be men. We are not like the Kitawala,* for the Kitawala only exists to teach hatred of the white man, it teaches how to kill those who have tried to destroy our souls. It is not a good thing, but the white man brought it on himself. In the old days there was the Anyota,† and other beliefs like it, which killed in times of trouble. But it only killed one or two, and only until such time as the deaths made people realize that they were going against the ancestors. When they realized this, and behaved as they should, the trouble ended and the killings ended. But the white man said the Anyota was evil, and the white man killed all the members it could find. And so the white man brought about a trouble that could only be ended, in some people's minds, by killing the white man himself. Our people do not believe like this, but we can understand it.

A man should behave the way he believes. To make someone else behave in a different way by pointing a gun at him, or by threatening him with a beating or with the box is evil, because it makes him less of a man, it makes him go against his beliefs; it makes him dishonest. Yet the white man says this is right. The white man has made it almost impossible for us to keep our beliefs, he makes us do bad things every day; he forces us to offend our ancestors. I do it myself, because I am afraid of the box. It is easier to plant the white man's cotton, to work for him on the roads, to treat him as though he were master of our souls as well as of our bodies. I hope the ancestors will understand and forgive.

I have tried to keep my dignity. I have tried to remain a man in the eyes of my father Whatever I may have done with my body, I have never betrayed my beliefs with my mind. But for my

---

* *A secret society of recent origin, primarily antiwhite. See p. 226.*

† *The leopard-man society, a traditional secret society. See pp. 221, 230 ff.*

children it is different. They do not know good and bad as I know it; the white man fills their heads with different ideas and they doubt. I circumcise my sons, but I can not circumcise their minds and their hearts. I can make their bodies acceptable, but they have to make their souls fit for the afterlife.

I have seen too much uncleanliness to have escaped its touch myself. But I have tried. And until I die, which can not be long, I shall keep trying, for myself and my people. After I am dead there will be no one left, unless somewhere I have planted a seed that has yet to grow and provide nourishment for those who live on. If I have done this, then maybe I too shall be thought fit to be given life at the side of my fathers."

5

The Teachers

In present-day Africa, even in the most remote areas, any full-blooded traditionalism is plainly unworkable. It is as plain to the nontraditionalists as it is to the would-be traditionalists. Matungi, as deeply as he believed that the way of tradition was better, by which he meant more moral because it was a way of life founded on principle rather than force, recognized the inevitable. The fact that he had begun to think in terms of personal salvation, of his own afterlife, rather than the afterlife of his people, is sufficient indication. His tradition, like most African traditions, concerns the people as a whole rather than individuals.

But the western world has brought change to every part of Africa, and the life and thought of the people has to adapt itself to these changes. Change has come with a vicious rapidity that has left little time for careful planning, and those who brought the change have themselves been caught in the same dilemma. To them it was more obvious than it was, at first, to the Africans that traditional ways were incompatible with the new order. Tribalism itself was unworkable from the administrative point of view. But all too often the newcomers thought that the establishment of artificial boundaries which included a miscellany of tribes was in itself an actual step toward unity. But nonetheless they realized that somehow the African had to be educated into the new way of life, that his horizons had to be broadened.

The early days were full of hope, for then man was thirsty for knowledge of new lands and new peoples. Perhaps he was less complacent about his own. But whatever the reason, in the dawn of the colonization of Africa, Europeans of several nationalities tried to discover all they could about the peoples they were colonizing. They were arduous days for the early settlers, yet even so many of them found time to make detailed and perceptive studies of the traditional ways of life around them. Administrators were primarily concerned with administering, yet it seemed reasonable to them to try and understand as much as they could about the people they governed.

But as the country opened up still further the demands of the administrative machinery became more complex, and adherence to the new regime was enforced, in the name of efficiency, and there was less attempt to understand the Africans. It became increasingly right, to the administrators, that nothing should be allowed to stand in their way. Ultimately efficient administration would bring benefits to the country and to the people, justifying their actions. Good government became the god of the immigrants, and traditions that stood in the way of that god were evil, and had to be eliminated. A new spirit of self-righteousness replaced the older and healthier spirit of adventure and inquiry. It was still a tolerant self-righteousness, but it grew surely into intolerance.

"Those dirty savages don't even try to appreciate what we are doing for them," grumbled a Belgian labor officer to me, idly flicking his whip. "We have given them good schools, we have put clothes on their backs, we have given them a chance to earn money and improve their standard of living, we are making their country one of the richest in the world, and they are not even grateful. You have to treat them like dogs."

He did. And no doubt he was one of the many who were surprised when the dog turned and bit its master. In fact, the Belgian government did not supply schools. It merely allowed them, exclusively Catholic mission schools to begin with, then Protestant;

it created new boundaries, carving the Congo up into denomina-
tional areas, as though tribal differences were not enough. The
clothes on the backs of the workers were rags cast at them by their
masters until such time as they could save enough from paltry
wages to buy a new shirt or a pair of cheap shorts. And with the
rags came a sense of shame in the human body, carefully inculcated
in all the mission schools where men and women and children were
taught to be more proud of clothes than of the body that God
gave them. The new standard of living was largely an opportunity
to be swindled by the multitudes of non-African storekeepers who
swept in like vultures to eat up the meager earnings of the new,
unwanted and, from the African point of view, unnecessary cash
economy. And if the Belgian Congo was becoming rich, its riches
were largely diverted to Belgian pockets, not African.

"Hang every one in ten!" shouted Colonel Grogan, of the
Kenya Legislative Council, for to the Kenya settler this was the
only language the bloody natives would understand. Yet Colonel
Grogan was a rather mild man. I had an entertaining luncheon
with him before I knew what or who he was. The only discordant
note during the meal was when he heard that I was going to visit
Makerere College, in Uganda, the only college in the whole of
East Africa where Africans could get anything more than a poor
high school education. "Just teaching a lot of stupid monkeys to
dress up like Europeans," he said. "Won't do any good. Just cause
a lot of discontent. They can never be like us, so better for them
not to try."

But there were others more calculating in their attitude. A mere
decade ago, when the question of federating the British territories
of Central Africa was being hotly discussed, Mr. Roy Welensky
was one of its most ardent champions. He was later knighted, and
became a prominent member of the federal government. In Northern Rhodesia he spoke with caution, so as not to inflame African
opinion unduly. Yet on a visit to England in 1952 he stated with

disarming candor that if federation succeeded, his immediate aim would be to double the number of the European population. The remarks of Sir Godfrey Huggins, Prime Minister of Southern Rhodesia, are even more revealing. Acclaimed as a great British Liberal, he also used some caution when faced with the possibility of antagonizing African opinion still further. But in London he felt free to say to a press conference: "There would be no Africans in a federal government. They are quite incapable of playing a full part . . . they may have a university degree, but their background is all wrong."

He also said: "It is time for the people in England to realize that the white man in Africa is not prepared and never will be prepared, to accept the African as an equal, either socially or politically." And, with even more naiveté he once asked, "Is there something in their [the Africans'] chromosomes which makes them more backward and different from peoples living in the East and West?" Since this represents an example of "liberalism" in Central Africa, it is no wonder that the Africans were skeptical of federation, and almost unanimously opposed it—to no effect. If we think of South Africa as intolerant, we should recognize that the same kind of intolerance, or worse, persisted throughout the continent wherever the white man set himself up over the black. It was necessary for the survival of the white, and this intolerance was one of the first things he taught, by his example, to the African. It is only remarkable that it took the African so long to learn the lesson and accept it. In places he still tries to reject it, but we can hardly be surprised when we occasionally, and rarely, hear the cry, "Africa for Africans." At least it makes more sense than "Africa for Europeans."

But it was before these thoughts of nationalism stirred the fires of discontent that the broad attitude to African education was formed, and it differed from one area to the other according to many factors. South Africa, with its policy of apartheid, or separate development, was free to develop what is still probably the most comprehensive educational system for its African population, with schools and universities giving opportunities for the full range of education available to the white population. This was possible because under apartheid the African can never be a competitor with the white population, from which he is so completely separated except when he chooses to be employed by whites. In East Africa, however, where segregation was a fact but not an official policy, and where the settlers felt far less secure in their position of supremacy, there was and still is strong opposition to giving the African any education that would ultimately put him on an equal footing with the white population. The university in Uganda is a happy exception, made possible only because Uganda was a crown protectorate and not a colony. For such men as Colonel Grogan and Godfrey Huggins do not really believe that the African is congenitally incapable of achieving the same standards as the European. If they did, they would not be driven by the fear of competition, as they are, into so violently opposing the granting of any opportunity for the African to prove himself. In their own hotbed of intolerance and fear they can not conceive that should the African achieve equality he might be less intolerant of the European than the European has been of him. As a result there has been an inexcusable paucity of schools and, until recently, no compulsory education for the African.

In West Africa there has never been any settler problem, and the Europeans have been able to afford to be more tolerant. Their attitude, however, has been that in the name of "efficient government" the African should be "enlightened," should become "evolved," one of the "elite." They have felt that the African should become as much like a European as his odd racial nature permits. Perhaps the French territories have been the most successful in this respect. In Belgian and Portuguese Africa the attitude has been rather to let the African continue to stew in his ignorance so long as it does not interfere with the government and with economic exploitation. For those who have enough sense to want to learn, the authorities have provided facilities up to a limited level. This policy has meant that in effect tribalism has continued to flourish, and the African population has remained content for a longer time than elsewhere. Unfortunately for the Belgians and Portuguese, however, this policy depended for success on complete isolation. And that became impossible. Rumors of developments in neighboring countries began to filter through and with them came notions of a new kind of freedom and liberty. Unhappily these notions were largely negative, from what I saw of them in the Congo. The tribal African there had little or no idea of national unity; his horizons were strictly those of the tribe. Stanleyville, Leopoldville, New York, Brussels, London all were simply "the great city" to him. Whether they were five hundred miles away or five thousand they were too remote to have any reality. And the tribal African in this area probably represents something like 80 per cent of the total population. So the new notions that fired off the explosion of discontent had nothing to do with any positive longing for national freedom. They were merely a recognition that there was something which others were being given and of which they were being deprived. There was a sudden, violent and highly volatile realization that they were being duped, that the degree of tribal freedom allowed by the Belgians, including the reluctant permission to continue with a very modified form of some initiation rites, was merely a way of keeping them ignorant and backward, so that they would be easier to handle.

Education, then, came with reluctance in all these areas, except possibly the west coast. When it came it was largely through missionary endeavor, and was confined to the lowest possible level. Coupled with the lack of practical opportunity this meant that the African really had no chance to show his ability, and equally no chance to understand this new world around him. And whereas in the earlier days there had been some attempt by the Europeans to understand the African, a new attitude quickly grew up, quaintly resentful, that the African simply did not know what was good for him, and if necessary he would have to be forced to accept western civilization, lock, stock and barrel, and like it. Any hesitancy on the part of Africans was taken as sheer stupidity or intellectual deficiency, and any resistance was taken as being founded in the same kind of intolerance that the European himself felt. Nobody seemed to consider that the African was perfectly capable of making up his own mind, or even had a right to. And nobody thought in terms of adaptation. It was all or nothing. It was merely a question of whether the African was capable of being civilized, or whether he was so biologically inferior that it was not worth the attempt. The few lonely voices that rang out in support of the African and his way of life and thought were ridiculed as being unrealistic and romantic. Nobody wanted to understand the African, or to grant that he had any legitimate say in the matter.

The lack of understanding was mutual and equally disastrous on both sides. It fomented ill will that was later to flare into unnecessary bloodshed. But the European, serene in the conviction that his way was as obviously right to the African as it was to himself, never stopped to consider the results of his actions, or how they might be interpreted by the Africans. The colonial history of Africa is full of the consequent calamities, mostly written off with bravado as "the good old days." In Ghana, then the Gold Coast, those good old days saw an attempt by the British to establish some kind of peaceful relationship with the powerful Ashanti confederation. A junior officer, attempting to cement an agreement by which the Ashanti recognized British rule to at least some extent, marched inland to their capital. There he demanded that he be allowed to sit on the Golden Stool. To him this was a throne, and as Her Majesty's representative it was his right to sit on it as a symbol of Her Majesty's seniority over the King of the

Ashanti. What he did not know was that the Golden Stool was not a throne, like the British throne, to be sat upon. It was the sacred symbol of the unity of the Ashanti nation, and it was believed to contain the soul of the Ashanti people. Therefore what the officer proposed **was not** merely to assert the supremacy of the British crown, but to defile the sacred stool, desecrate the soul of the nation, and so destroy its very existence. Not unnaturally he was refused, took this as a deliberate insult, and so the last and bloodiest war between the Ashanti and the British began through mutual ignorance.

In Kenya, early settlers thought that by offering payment they could buy land and acquire full title to it. If the Africans were willing to accept a few shillings for several hundred acres that was their business. This, so to speak, was the British tribal custom.

But the African understanding was different. By their custom land can never be sold, but the usufruct can. When they accepted money from the settlers they thought they were merely selling the right to the fruit of the land. The earth itself could not be sold because it did not belong to the living; it belonged to the people of the tribe, past, present, and yet to come. The Kikuyu and Masai were the tribes in question, and to them the land was as sacred as was the Golden Stool to the Ashanti. Later, when the Europeans began to desecrate the land by digging it up and building on it, and then when they refused to acknowledge that the original owners had any rights at all over it, both parties were convinced that the others were liars and cheats. The settlers had by then invested large amounts of money and labor in what they considered to be their property, and had no intention of giving it up, but the Africans' resentment went far deeper than the mere loss of the land. They had unwittingly committed the gravest of offenses against the ancestors by allowing the desecration of the soil on which their fathers had been born, lived and died and in which they were buried and still lived, in the afterworld. And worst of all, they had been forced to give up the land not in manly battle (as they had acquired it), but by what seemed to them deliberate trickery.

Even so the subsequent resentment might have been avoided, because of the African's acceptance that the white man's customs were different from his own, had it not been for two further factors, neither of which can be excused on grounds of misunderstanding. The first was governmental attitude to the land question. Oddly enough the first formal protests about appropriation came not from the Africans (they had no political voice) but from the Indian community. Indians had been imported to work on the East African railway, and had gradually grown into a wealthy trading community. Within the first few years of European settlement the Indians saw that the coveted Highlands of Kenya, over 16,000 square miles, were being regarded as a white reserve. On their objection the following reply was made by the then Deputy Commissioner of the East African Protectorate:

"You are in error in assuming that the Government has any intention of drawing a distinction between Europeans and Indians as far as rights of mining, settling and acquiring land are concerned."

But one year later, when an Indian purchased the estate of a bankrupt white settler, Lord Delamere raised violent objections and proposed that the entire Highlands area be made an exclusively white reservation. He was appointed as Chairman of the Land Commission which, three years later, recommended precisely that.

A complaint was made to the British Secretary of State, but Lord Elgin had already made up his mind, and voiced his opinion in the following roundabout way:

"It is not consonant with the views of His Majesty's Government to impose legal restrictions on any particular section of the community, but as a matter of administrative convenience grants [of land] should not be made to Indians in the Uplands area."

Taking courage from this, the Kenya Legislative Council (all white) appointed a committee which advocated that "No restriction be placed on free transfer and dealings in land except where parties concerned are of different communities, when the power of veto should be retained." In this way segregation and serious economic and social disabilities became the practice in Kenya, not as law, but as "administrative convenience," or, as another explanation worded it, because "The interests of the community must be considered before those of the individual."

One of the final acts was an Order in Council issued by the British crown, in 1939, securing the Highlands exclusively, and legally, for the white community. As a result some ten million acres were occupied by three to four thousand settlers, while the little remaining good land, a fifth of that occupied by whites, had to suffice for a million Kikuyu. The rest of the land, for the other millions of Kenya's African population, is ridden by the tsetse fly, and virtually useless.

Apart from the manner in which land was alienated, the other factor that led to bitter resentment was the fact that while "liberal" settlers proclaimed that if the Kikuyu and the Masai had been allowed to continue their ways the land would have been ruined by their primitive farming techniques, they did nothing to teach them how to farm better. There was, evidently, no prospect at all of ever having even a share in the land that had once been theirs. And so, Mau-Mau.

And it was not only in respect to land that education was deliberately withheld. While the Europeans did little to learn about the people they were governing they also did little to enlighten them about the civilization they claimed they were bringing to Africa. Such government education as existed was designed to fulfill certain needs: the needs of the European community. Literate Africans were useful in many ways, although too much literacy was considered dangerous and undesirable. A certain amount of technical training was essential to provide a body of cheap semiskilled labor, but it could not be allowed to continue beyond a given standard or the Africans would soon be competing with the whites. This led to odd situations in different territories. Thus the train running from the Belgian Congo into Rhodesia had to stop at the border so that a white engine driver could take over from the Belgian black, because in Rhodesia his job was classed as skilled, and reserved for whites. And a South Rhodesian white caused great hilarity in a North Rhodesian mine by demanding, as his right, a job as truck driver, because to him that was a white man's job. He had applied for any job at the mine, and been told there were none. Then he saw an African driving a truck and demanded his job. The mine manager, not without certain humor, called the African driver in and said that the white Bwana wanted his job, he would be given another. He then signed on the white Bwana and told him that the particular job he had requested was to take the truck and clear out the African latrines.

Unfortunately men like the mine manager are rare, and insofar as the Africans have learned by the behavior of their masters they have not been edified or encouraged, and the few government schools have not done much to help. But if the government did not set up more than a handful of schools, the missions did. In the Congo all the schools were run by missions of various denominations, but these were also only able to provide a limited education, and the teachers were as steeped in the conviction of their moral superiority as were the settlers in their political and physical superiority. A few early missionaries did great pioneer work in really probing the African consciousness and the workings of African society, but they were outnumbered by the many who wanted nothing to do with savage customs, and who would not defile themselves by even learning about them. I have met American and British missionaries who have spent up to thirty years in the French-speaking Congo, but who have not bothered to learn a word of French. They were not concerned with the world around them, merely with the world they created for themselves. And although these same missionaries have learned the languages of the Africans, sometimes to perfection, they know nothing of the people. They consider them evil through and through, and think that the only way to deal with them is to cast out everything that is past, sprinkle water over them and start all over again. Yet the Africans among whom they were working were the same people whom another missionary, with a very different outlook, refused to convert, because they did not as yet know what evil was. Before conversion he would have to teach them the meaning of sin. He preferred, he said, to live among them, trying to understand their world, finding the good in it, and building on that by his own example.

But with the majority of missions the work of teaching had to begin with the work of destruction: the total destruction of all old beliefs, the total destruction of all old ways, followed by the initial teaching that man is evil—particularly the black man. The missionaries said that only by clearing away the savagery and fear and superstition of the tribal African could they prepare that people for conversion to Christianity, the religion of love in which all men, as children of the one God, are brothers. But much of the savagery was in their own minds, in their own violently narrow way of looking at a strange new world, in their own inability and unwillingness to understand. The fear was *their* fear, a fear of the unknown. They believed that they were dealing with the forces of evil, and in that belief they became savage themselves. They unleashed a spiritual holocaust that all but destroyed not only the spiritual life of the Africans, but even the deep foundations in which it had its roots. It is small wonder that in the place of the traditional beliefs so destroyed there grew up a pitiful imitation of the belief of the missionary, a belief that the ways and thoughts of foreigners are savage and superstitious, and can only be counteracted with savagery. The African, thus taught, applied the same theory to the Europeans. This was the beginning of real savagery in Africa, the beginning of real fear, and real hatred—born out of a religion of love and brotherhood.

It was the Portuguese who first established Christianity in Africa south of the Sahara. From their trading posts they colonized and converted. The great Congo kingdom became Christian in the sixteenth century, but after a couple of centuries it reverted, retaining only the superficialities of the new religion, symbols that are even today incorporated in some of the Congo fetishes. The glass of a reliquary was, for instance, considered as a magical means of reflecting evil. The Madonna and Child was plainly a powerful fertility magic. And perhaps the most powerful magic of all was the mysterious devouring of the flesh and blood of Bwana Yesu. When Portuguese power waned and their control over the BaKongo was broken, the old beliefs reasserted themselves easily, and to them were added variants of these new features.

The same thing happens every day in contemporary Africa. The administrator can force a change in the way of living. He can force men to work for money and to pay taxes and to have only one wife and not to kill those who would kill him. But the missionary can not force a change in belief. All he can do is to sow the seeds of mistrust, destroy faith in the old beliefs, and then hope that the new belief will replace them. But it seldom does. The African may adopt the outer form of Christianity as a symbol of his sophistication, or as a convenience because it may make him more acceptable to the government, or because it is expedient, providing an opportunity for an education and for a job from which he would otherwise be barred. But this does not mean that he sees Christianity as the missionaries would have him see it. Except in the urban areas where the Africans have had at least some opportunity for acquiring a thorough education and a western rationale, the African has no background against which he can understand the theory of Christian theology. All he can do is to assess it from his own immediate point of view, against his own background, and judge it by the living example of those who teach it. On neither count does he find much to be said in its favor.

He finds that its teachings are largely incomprehensible, and that its practice deprives a man of his adulthood, making him unacceptable to the ancestors. He finds it has little to add to his own moral code, its commandments being mere repetitions of his own; such as the injunctions not to kill, not to steal, not to sleep with another man's wife. He is not likely to worship any God but his own, and as for making graven images, who are the missionaries to talk? They pretend that they have seen God and they put up images of him all over the place, and even hang them around their necks. To take the name of the tribal God in vain is punishable by tribal lore, and brings the curse of leprosy or death, so there is nothing new in that commandment either. As for worshiping one's God only one day in seven, the Africans feel it is better to remember him every day. They ask how a God can be remembered on one day and forgotten on six. The African honors his father and mother, and has his own rules against murder, adultery and theft. And as for bearing false witness against your neighbors, or coveting their property, those are among the greatest sins of tribal society. This is not to say that the African keeps to his code any better than the Europeans, though in many respects he does. The African merely points out that the European, even the missionary, is not particularly good at keeping to his own code. So what do the Christians really have to offer? Love, brotherhood, freedom from fear? Example does not show it.

It is when the African judges the religion of the white man by the behavior of its professional exponents, let alone by the behavior of its lay members, that he not only loses faith in Christianity but he begins to suspect it as some kind of secret, magical weapon designed to place him even more fully under the white man's control. The African respects truth, but he sees no truth in the lives of many of the missionaries. How can they talk about brotherhood when they fight among each other, call each other unbelievers, and even refuse to enter each others' churches? A not unusual example is Bangui, now in the Central African Republic, but still in the French Congo the last time I was there, in 1957. At that time there was not only the usual difference of opinion between Catholics and Protestants, hard enough for the missionaries to explain to the Africans. But there were two Baptist missions, within a few miles of each other, both English-speaking. They not only prevented their adult converts from mixing with each other, but they prevented the children to whom they were teaching the doctrine of love and brotherhood from playing with the other children, and further taught them that the others were following false gods. The missionaries themselves would not talk to each other. All because one practiced baptism by total immersion, the other by partial immersion.

In the urban areas the Africans have additional cause for mistrust. For if Christianity is truly a religion of love and brotherhood, why should there be separate services for black and white, with the texts for the African services stressing the virtues of loyalty of servants to masters? And if it is a large town or city, there are often separate churches, or even separate chapels in the same church. How does this fit in, the African asks, with the doctrine of love and brotherhood? It so happens that the notion of brotherhood has widespread and deep-seated roots throughout Africa, based on a profound respect for the family, around which African society revolves. But the African notion of brotherhood involves strong injunctions as to responsibilities as well as to rights and privileges. So an African Christian feels his obligations in this regard deeply, but at the same time expects reciprocal respect. He can not be overly enthusiastic about his new faith when he does not get it.

The same divorce between preaching and practice is even more apparent when the African looks at the Europeans engaged in government, business or industry all around him. These men are not preachers, but there are many who lose no opportunity for preaching. The educated African is sensible enough not to judge the ways of Europeans by African standards, but he feels perfectly within his rights in judging Europeans by their own professed standards. The earlier settler he could understand, and he could submit to him with more dignity because he had proved his superiority and backed it with force. The earlier settlers were men of vision, men of determination, and they were often dedicated men. They believed in something, and they tried to live up to those beliefs. Even if the African did not agree with them he respected them for their consistency. But later waves of immigrants, of missionaries as well as laymen, did not bring the same kind of dedication. At first they brought adventurers, and then a whole flood of semi-educated nonentities who only came to Africa because they would have been failures anywhere else. At least in Africa they were white.

These people also taught, by their example. They taught how to lie and cheat. They opened themselves, and through themselves the whole white race, to contempt. The simple, honest-thinking villager, unaccustomed to seeing in circles and around corners, saw the lie at once. He saw the immorality among the Europeans, the lying and cheating of each other, which at first was lightly disguised but soon became flagrant and open. He saw the deceit in constantly unfulfilled promises. And he perceived in his same direct way a great lack of dignity and manhood, for a man does not lie to another man; he stands where he stands and does not pretend he is standing elsewhere.

As far as possible the African stood aloof, but where the two worlds impinged there was only one thing for him to do, as the European did not respect his honesty, and that was to reply in kind. After all, had he not been told that in order to better his chances he should become as much like the white man as possible? So he too, when brought into this situation, became a liar and a cheat, an adulterer and thief, a murderer, and a worshiper of strange gods whose names were daily taken in vain. The Day of God became the day of greatest opportunity for lying and cheating and stealing and killing and sleeping with other men's wives. Coveting one's neighbor's property became second nature, as the Europeans occupied all the best land and the best jobs, taking from the African anything he wanted, including his self-respect.

But though the Europeans could steal his land, steal the strange wealth that lay beneath its surface, and exercise their rights as conquerors to exploit human labor, they could never steal the African's soul because they could never win his respect. The early settlers might have done it, for they were men, but the weaklings that followed were no more than animals in African eyes—unpredictable, untrustworthy, deceitful, occasionally bloodthirsty and savage, and with no more respect for each other than they had for themselves. They were worse than animals, for animals have no souls, and they do not have the power of speaking and thinking and feeling in the way of human beings. These white man-animals *did* have this power, and they deliberately misused it. They used speech to tell lies, thought to deceive, and feeling to hate.

This is what the African was taught.

6

The Man of God

"When I was a boy I was godless. I was born into a poor family, and I saw little of my father or mother. They both had to work during the day, and when they returned at night it was only to get drunk and to swear at each other. At an early age I used to go out with other children, and I soon learned their evil ways. I did things that make me ashamed when I think of them, even today. And yet then I thought that my life was better than that of my parents, because it was more exciting and adventurous. I sank lower and lower, and my only ambition was to get away from home and be on my own.

As soon as I was old enough to leave school I took a job in a factory, and I was content with that. But one weekend an evangelist mission visited the town and out of curiosity I went to watch them as they held their service on the street corner. I remember liking the brass band, and I found myself joining the crowd in order to get closer. Then I found myself not only listening to the music, but also listening to the preacher. He was talking about the work of his Mission in Africa, of all the souls they were saving from heathen darkness, and of their great medical and educational work. He said that even among us there were heathens that needed to be saved, and I felt him looking at me. The band began playing again and I was filled with a longing to go down on my knees and admit my guilt. But I waited until the crowd broke up, and then I left and went back to my old and sinful life.

It was several months later that I heard a band playing, one Sunday morning, on the same street corner. In that moment my life changed, because during these months I had been filled with uncertainty. My life had seemed more worthless than ever, yet this had only made me seek after worldly pleasures all the more. But the moment I heard the music on the street corner I knew why I felt as I did. The Lord had called me once, and I had refused Him. Now He was calling me again, begging me to save my own life and let Him help me. I ran to where the Mission was holding its service, and fell on my knees and proclaimed myself a sinner.

It was a glorious moment. A great wave of relief came over me, the darkness lifted and I was flooded with light and warmth. I heard the preacher asking me if I wanted salvation enough to give up my own life for it, and I cried, 'Yes, yes, I want to give my life to my Lord, if He will have it.' As I spoke those words I suddenly realized that I was not only being saved, I was being called on to save others. I could see in my mind the shores of Africa, and the dark forests far inland, peopled with heathens who needed me.

I joined the Mission, and left my home for good. I had to make a complete break, even though my family did not understand it and begged me not to go. But I wanted everyone to share the joy that I had found, and I went down on my knees and prayed for them, that they too might be saved. More and more I could hear the Lord calling me to save others just as I had been saved. But my parents still rejected salvation, and rejected Christ. I left home full of sadness for them, but I told them I would never again cross their threshold until they accepted Christ. For all these years I have never been back; but a few months ago I heard that my father had at last admitted his sins and followed the Lord. He died in peace a few days later, blessing me for my prayers.

Life at the Mission headquarters was difficult, for my body was not used to the restrictions I wanted to place on it. But soon my mind became so occupied with other things that even bodily desires and the lusts of the flesh left me. I met missionaries who had worked in Africa, and began to learn what my new life would be like. I was trained for the work, and all the time I heard Christ calling me to the heathen. But still I had to fight my old self, and it was several months before my past life became a forgotten nightmare.

As soon as my training was complete I volunteered for work in the field, and within two weeks I was on my way to Mombasa. Most of the trip I spent in the company of other missionaries, learning still more from them, and preparing myself inwardly for my new life. I took a train to Kampala, in Uganda, and there I was met by a Mission car which drove me through to the border, and into the Belgian Congo. It was a rough trip, taking nearly two weeks, and I had to fight a sense of nausea at some of the sights I saw. In one village there was a wedding party, a whole line of women exposing their breasts in front of the men, with the unfortunate bride in the middle, painted in white, practically naked. I was told that she had no choice in the matter, and that she would be married to an old man with half a dozen other wives. It was horrible. None of the people seemed to have anything in the way of clothes; even the adults went barefoot, and the children, boys and girls alike, were naked and playing with each other freely. They were festering with sores and the villages were filthy. Whenever we stopped we were surrounded by these creatures, and the smell was so terrible I just had to try and hold my breath. They reached out their hands, eaten by leprosy, and would have taken hold of mine if I had not pulled away. They seemed to have no sense of their indecency or of their own uncleanliness.

Shortly after crossing into the Congo we entered the forest, and for the first time I felt real fear. It was not fear of the savages, for I had no cause to worry about my bodily safety. I had committed myself in trust to the Lord, and He would look after me. I felt fear for another reason, fear for the people who lived in the forest, fear of the immensity of the task I had undertaken. For the forest was evil. I felt it as soon as I saw it, stretching away into the distance, far out of sight. As we drove down from the hills it closed in above us and I could sense the presence of evil all around. It was even on the faces of the natives as they came to stare at us from the roadside. It was everywhere. On either side of the road the forest was so thick that I could see no more than the very edge; beyond that it was dark and impenetrable. The trees were so high that the only time we could really see the sky was when we came to a village, where the forest had been cut down by the natives for their plantations.

I made up my mind that I would make it my work to bring the heathen out of the forest, to give them sunlight, to show them how to live in God's open world, to teach them to abandon this darkness, and I took courage from my resolution and gloried in God each time we came to a clearing where I could see the sky and the sun.

When we finally reached the Mission station I was shocked to find that it looked no different from the native compounds all around. It sat in a small clearing, with the forest close behind, not more than a stone's throw. The buildings looked exactly like native huts; mud walls and the roofs thatched with leaves and sticks. Of course I was prepared for hardship, and it was not the prospect of discomfort that upset me, it was rather that I felt we should be setting an example to the natives, showing them how they should be living, not ourselves living like them.

The head of the Mission at that time was an old man, and he had one of his servants show me my house. Like the others it had mud walls and a leaf roof, but I was surprised on going inside to find how clean and cool it was. It was simply furnished, and although the curtains and bedding all had a smell of mold about them I was almost trapped into acceptance. I did not want anything more, my own tastes were simple and this was better than anything I had ever had at home. But I had been warned how easy it was to accept the ways of the heathens and fail to set them an example in all matters. I had been taught that in everything I did I must set an example. After I had washed, as best as I could with a single bowl of cold water, I went back to the main building and talked with the Reverend Lewis. I spoke my mind freely, and he explained the difficulties of making any more elaborate arrangements for washing and toilet facilities. He agreed that we should set the natives a good example in these matters, as in others, but he pointed out that until he had come they had not even used the outside privies that most native compounds now boasted, they had merely relieved themselves in the forest, like animals.

I had a great deal to learn, and my impatience and intolerance lessened as my understanding grew. I thought that it would be largely a matter of showing the natives a better way of life, and that with that example they would readily come to accept the Lord. But I quickly learned that the heathen superstitions and savage customs were deeply embedded in centuries of darkness and ignorance. The dead were condemned to everlasting damnation, but the living were there to be saved, and I knew that every death of an unconverted heathen from now on would be on my conscience. Yet they were blinded by the evil all around them, and by the teachings of men like Matungi. As I began my work of teaching the Gospel of Christ I found myself up against a blank wall, as impenetrable as the forest itself. I set every example I could, living simply, worshiping publicly, but all to no effect, so it seemed. Even Matungi would listen, politely enough, but with no understanding. And when I had finished he, like the others, would go away and continue in his old ways just as before.

After about a year, when I was more familiar with the language and did not have always to use interpreters, I asked for permission to visit some of the neighboring villages and bring them the Gospel. The Reverend Lewis gave me Amboko, whom we had just made one of our catechists, and I took two servants to help with setting up camp or whatever might be necessary that way as well as for cooking and washing clothes. I was away for three months, and in that time I saw more evil than I had ever thought possible. Most of the time I had to sleep in a native hut, because Amboko told me it would be unsafe outside in a tent. The huts were not, as I had imagined, like those in which we lived at the Mission, except from the outside. They had no windows, and were pitch black inside, even at midday. They were filled with spiders and lice, and although I always had my hut cleaned out and thoroughly disinfected I never managed to get rid of the smell, and after a few days the insects would crawl back in again.

But that was not what worried me so much as the life of the people. I had never believed that the force of Satan could pervert God's creatures so utterly. The men and women were immoral in every way. They slept with each other before they were married, they took more than one wife, and they practiced all sorts of heathen rites on each other. God knows how terrible they were, I could never bring myself to watch them. All I saw were some of their dances, which like their whole lives were filled with a sexual lust they gratified openly in front of the children, encouraging them to imitate their vile actions, without the slightest thought for God.

Yet when I began to teach them they merely responded that this was their way, and that I did not understand it. I read them the word of God to show them that He Himself taught that these things were evil, but they were blind even to the Gospel. I kept my faith, however, and every day I would stand out in the open, with Amboko and my two servants, and hold prayers. I prayed for the heathen that they might see the light that I was offering them for Christ, and I found some peace in the thought that my prayers would not go unheard. But at the end of three months I knew I had made not a single convert. There were those who would listen, and who would agree that it was bad to steal, and bad to kill, and bad to sleep with other men's wives, but they still refused to accept Christ as their Saviour.

It was when I returned to the Mission from that trip that I realized that this was something else that I would have to resign myself to, and that I would have to carry the burden of these people's sins for my life, for failing to save them. But I also realized that it was in part my own youthful enthusiasm that had led me away too fast. The Reverend Lewis had known what would happen, but he also knew I would have to learn the lesson myself. I had seen the light so clearly, and heard His voice calling me, I could not understand why others could not come to believe, just as I did. I felt there was only one thing to do, and that was to begin with the children, and hope that through them I might be able to reach their parents.

I did not get the chance right away, as the Reverend Lewis looked after the Mission School himself. But after I had been at the Mission for several years he decided to go home on long leave, and I took charge, with Amboko as my right-hand man. He was a gift, I thought then, from God Himself. He had little influence with the adults, but he could do almost anything with the children. Within a few weeks of the Reverend Lewis' departure the school had nearly twice the number of children, and although they came mainly because of the meals we gave them, and sometimes food to take home to their parents, I knew we were doing the right thing. At least we had them there, and we could talk to them and teach them the way of the Lord. They heard the Lord's word day after day, and with Amboko's help they soon learned the catechism. I began to teach them to sing the songs I had myself learned back at the Mission headquarters, and I hoped that one day I would be able to have a band. I wrote to the Reverend Lewis to ask him to bring back some musical instruments with him for this purpose, but before my letter reached him he had died of a heart attack. I was appointed head of the Mission, and was told that as soon as possible

I would be sent an assistant. Meanwhile I had to carry on by myself.

Those were lonely days, without anyone to talk to in a civilized tongue. Headquarters refused my request for instruments, saying they had little enough money to support their own bands. I felt that our need was greater, but there was nothing I could do. I began to realize that I was really on my own when after my evening meal was finished I sat by myself on the veranda of my hut, looking at the stars. The Reverend Lewis and I had talked of many things at such times, and though we did not always agree he had been a great comfort to me. Several times I tried to talk to Amboko, but as soon as the day was over he seemed to want to go back to his family, as though our work ended at nightfall. In any case he was difficult to talk to, and I was afraid of trying to discuss the Bible with him as his understanding was limited. Several times I caught him misinterpreting the Word, and once he even argued with me in front of the children that his interpretation was as good as mine. After that I never felt I could quite trust him as I had done, and I began to wonder if I had not already trusted him too much.

I found an excuse to take him off school work, so he was not so much in contact with the children. They too had grown less respectful, and I realized that I had been too lax. I took over all the teaching myself, and set Amboko to work in charge of a building project I had had in mind for some while. I had thought it would keep me occupied and give me something to think about instead of always turning my thoughts home. More and more I found myself wondering what was going on at home, but I had no one to write to there except the Mission, as my own family still refused to accept Christ as their Saviour. So during the daytime I taught at the school, and in the late afternoons I inspected the clearing work that had been done.

It was wonderful to see the forest coming down on all sides. I could feel the power of Satan receding as every tree fell. In a matter of months we had about ten acres cleared completely, and God's sunshine lit on the land for the first time. In the evenings I worked on my plans for the buildings. I wanted them to be as different from the heathen huts as possible, but Amboko put up an objection to almost every plan I made. He did not even like cutting down the forest, he said it would bring misfortune, unless we were going to use the ground for plantations. But I wanted the plantations to be outside the mission compound. He said we should leave at least some trees standing for shade, and for the protection of the soil, and I suppose he was right, but I just felt that I wanted every tree down.

During the beginning of this work I had sent some photographs back to the headquarters, with a letter explaining what I was doing, and telling of my plans for building a modern school with a gymnasium, and with playing fields where the children could learn healthy sports. They published the letter, and also my subsequent letters showing how progress was being made. Before long my prayers were answered and money began to come in from all sides. With this money I was able to buy bricks from Matadi, and later tiles, and I was able to give employment to the parents of my school children in the cutting of lumber. Within two years I had six new brick buildings, including a new house for myself, a school building, an assembly building, a kitchen, and two dormitories, one for boys and one for girls. At this point my assistant arrived, and was able to help me finish the project.

He had a young wife with him, and although I had not been happy about this when I first heard of it, at least I could now offer them decent living quarters. They moved into the house I had built for myself, and for the time I lived in an office in the assembly building. They soon took to the work, and I found the woman to be as devoted a Christian as her husband. In six months I felt able to leave them in charge while I went back home for my first leave. I did not go because I needed any rest; on the contrary I was more filled with energy than ever. But I felt that I could raise still further interest, and headquarters arranged a lecture tour for me. I prayed that it would be a success, and once more my prayers were answered. After a year I returned to Africa with more helpers, including the woman who is now my wife.

The Mission grew and flourished, our school was full, and we were always able to employ a number of the parents for the upkeep of the buildings and the grounds. We tried to make gardens and fill them with flowers, but they soon withered and died. The baked earth made admirable tennis courts, though, and this became a welcome relaxation for the staff. I knew that I was living well, probably in far greater comfort than I could ever have afforded at home. But I felt this was deserved, and even needed if I was to keep on with the work, which increased every day. We now had a hospital as well as the school. And it was good to be able to relax and forget for a while that one was in Africa, surrounded by heathens. I had tried to make friends with them, but that was impossible, and it always will be, at least for many years to come. Also I began to find just how little I could trust them.

In all sorts of ways they seemed deliberately to try and upset my plans, to cause annoyances and difficulties. Particularly Amboko, who once had been our most trusted catechist. In the kitchens they used to give away food without my permission, to all their friends and relatives. When I chided them they asked me if I had not taught them to share whatever they had, that more would always be given them by the Lord. Our building supplies disappeared in spite of being kept under lock and key. The books and pencils we bought for our children were to be found on sale in markets many miles away. Servants would take holidays without permission, and even when they were at work they were incurably lazy and could not be trusted to do anything. I found I had to check to see that every little thing I had ordered to be done had actually been done. And above all, although every single person on the station was a Christian—it was a condition of employment—I had to threaten to fine them if they did not come to church.

It all began to get on my nerves, and I asked myself if this was really what the Lord had called me to do. I knew that it was not. I talked it over with my wife and we both decided to spend several years in the villages around us. It had always been my ambition to convert Matungi, though I knew it to be hopeless, and we made Ndola one of our chief objectives. But the capita, Masoudi, who should have been our strength, was a renegade and had abandoned his faith. Matungi offered help, but it was in an attempt to deceive us, and we had to set up our headquarters at a government rest house a few miles away. I brought Amboko with us, because I felt that I had perhaps not shown enough trust and faith myself, and he seemed anxious to be of help. We took only three others to help with the housework and cooking, and to help my wife with her medical work.

There were several men at Ndola who had been converted to Christianity, but they came from distant villages and belonged to different faiths. I felt it was better to have nothing to do with them, although they were welcome to attend my church services if they wanted to. But they never did, not once. There was only one who belonged to us; he had been one of the Reverend Lewis' first converts, a man named Isaaka, who had a young son, Ibrahimo. He was a good Christian, and regularly attended my church; but he never brought his wife, and seldom his son. He said that his wife refused to become a Christian, and his son, although he had been baptized, did not want to come. This was bad enough, but when I tried to get Masoudi to exert his influence he said he could do nothing, it was a matter for Matungi, the witch doctor.

It seemed that Matungi was about to have one of his heathen initiations that come about once every three years, and that he wanted Ibrahimo to enter. In this initiation the boys are cruelly circumcised and taught all manner of evil practices, including the act of sex. I could not allow it, and although Ibrahimo protested that he wanted to join the initiation I knew that it was merely the devil speaking in his mouth, and I persuaded Isaaka to take him back to my mission hospital and have him circumcised there. I went to Ndola and called all the villagers together, including Matungi, and told them what I had done. I told them that Ibrahimo was a Christian, and could not take part in their heathen rites. I also told them that it was not necessarily our custom to circumcise, that I had not been circumcised myself, but as it was so important to them I had arranged to have Ibrahimo circumcised at the hospital.

I still do not see what more I could have done; it was more than I wanted to do, for circumcision at the age of eleven or twelve is a cruel thing even under the best conditions. But I was afraid that if I did not do it, sooner or later Matungi would get Ibrahimo. I had to avoid that at any cost. But instead of understanding, the villagers, led by Matungi, said that I had done an evil thing. For a while I thought they were going to attack me, but I was prepared to die for the Lord, and was not afraid. I told them that what I had done was not evil, that it was the work of the Lord, and that I was a man of God. At this, Matungi, with a blasphemy I hate to repeat, said in a loud voice, 'I too am a man of God.'

Matungi turned the hearts of all the villagers away from me. When Isaaka and his son returned, some months later, Matungi ordered his followers not to talk to them; even the children refused to talk to Ibrahimo. And now, whenever I tried to talk to anyone in the village they just laughed at me, and laughed at the Word of God. And that was not all. There was only one person in whom I could confide. I needed help, I needed desperately to know where I had gone wrong, how I could reach these heathen and save them from damnation. I could not talk to my wife; her work was mainly in the hospital, and she did not understand these things. The only person was Amboko. I turned to Amboko, and once more gave him my trust, and told him of my need. He tried to avoid me as he had been doing for some time, but I ordered him to come to the guest house one evening and we sat together on the veranda.

I felt that this is what I should have done more often; I had learned so much from the Reverend Lewis in this way, could not Amboko learn from me in the same way? I confided in him, and asked him why it was that I could not win the respect of Matungi and the people of Ndola, why they would not listen to the Word of God. He remained stubbornly silent, and I was suddenly filled with a dreadful loathing for him. I felt that old presence of evil suddenly welling up all around me until I wanted to cry out. It was as though the forest had suddenly grown right back over my life, and was crushing me beneath it. Amboko stood up and asked me if it was true that I had not been circumcised. When I answered yes, he spat at me, his filthy spittle clinging to my clothes as I stood numb with shock, and said, 'That is what we think of the uncircumcised.'

Perhaps it was a humiliation I needed. My wife and I returned to our Mission the next day, and I felt a great relief come over me as I saw once again those clean, Christian faces and those clean Christian buildings. I gathered the staff all together and we prayed for Amboko's soul.

I never saw him again, though I was told that he had gone back to his own village, and had completely renounced his Christian faith. But I have not forgotten him, and he serves as a lesson for us that the devil is all around us, even among those whom we think are our own. Every Sunday when I preach in church I look down on that sea of smiling black faces and wonder how many Ambokos there are among them. I wonder how many of them are there merely because we feed them and clothe them and give them an education and keep them healthy.

As far as possible I try to keep the children from their parents, because I know that we can trust none of the older ones. If we are to save the children at all we must give them every chance to grow up among true Christians, even if it means parting them from their heathen families. Perhaps the older ones can not be blamed too harshly; they have grown up from infancy in an atmosphere of evil, they do not know any different, they are too old to learn. But I know that my job is to bring the Word to these children, to *make* them understand. If they ignore the Word they deserve to be damned. I have given my life to bring them salvation. I thought I could bring them a new way of life as well, show them how to live like us. But they continue to live in their filth. If you put windows in their huts they block them up, they prefer to defecate in the forest rather than in the latrines we have built for them, I now know that almost every boy either has attended or will attend the initiation school and be circumcised according to their ungodly rites, and I know that there are many things that I do *not* know about. All I can say is that the Lord called me here to spread his Word. If I have failed to bring many truly to Christ, at least I have shown them the way and given them the Word. If they choose to reject it, their blood is not on my hands but on theirs, and on the hands of the Evil One who is in them all."

7

The Taught

The story of the Reverend Henry Spence that has just been given is not intended to be representative. It was told to me in a mood that fluctuated between anger and despair. And it is specific to the village of Ndola. I have met missionaries, none of them quite like Henry Spence, but many of them sharing both his anger and his despair, and many of them taking refuge in a far more bitter self-righteousness than his. The point is that the feelings of the Africans with whom they come in contact are generally reciprocal.

There was a Catholic priest, an Italian, who had lived in the same forest area as Spence for over a quarter of a century. He was dedicated to the betterment of mankind, and it seemed to me, though perhaps Father Longo would not agree, that he was more concerned with this goal than he was with the baptism of converts. At this mission, in the village of Nduye, it was almost impossible to tell who was Christian and who was not. Muslims, Pagans and Christians alike joined together in a labor of love—the building of a new Mission church. At the consecration, one Ascension Day, as Father Longo was saying the Mass, a host of pagan pygmies came in from the forest, bearing gifts of forest flowers and leaves and fruits, and danced into the church to make their offering. Then they stood at the back of the church, chattering happily, until the Mass was over, when they danced their heathen way back to their heathen forest, full of love and gratitude to Father Longo for the love and kindness he had shown them over the years. In return for the respect he had shown for their ways they gave him their respect, and although none of these Pygmy men and women were converts, they had learned what Father Longo had come to teach them.

There was a Calvinist minister at Bangui, sent there to try and establish some kind of liaison between the various Protestant churches in the French Congo. It was at Bangui that the two Baptist churches were not on speaking terms. The Reverend Chaptal was considered odd because he welcomed anyone into his church, and was thought subversive because he preached that there is one God, and all of us, Christian or otherwise, are striving toward the same goal, each in our own way, all equally loved by that one God. Further, the Reverend Chaptal was an example of everything he preached. As a result, in this modern city, his home and his church became a symbol, among a confused and politically unhappy community, of a higher truth and goodness.

But there are the others who are more interested in themselves and in their own ideas than they are in mankind. They are as unable as they are unwilling to see anything except what they want to see, and they bring only unhappiness and disillusionment, skepticism and bitterness. They give their respect, insofar as they give it at all, only to their fellow believers; for the rest of mankind, the vast majority born into other beliefs, these missionaries feel varying emotions from noninterest to consuming hatred.

Laymen equally teach by their example, and the nature of the African's acceptance of our western world is markedly different in urban and rural communities. In the town the outer acceptance is all that counts, and that is easy enough to assume. The western pattern of life is already established, and the adoption of Christianity falls as naturally into place as does the custom of being seen in church every Sunday. The traditionalist or extremist who does not assume this symbol of sophistication stands out prominently, but among all town dwellers lies the basic unity of skepticism and spiritual emptiness. In the village, however, the important factor is inner acceptance. Outwardly it would be difficult to tell a Christian from a pagan, but the two are divided by the unbridgeable gulf between their beliefs.

In the towns there is virtually no belief, only a way of life that the majority accept. There is no belief because in being forced to abandon traditional beliefs, in being taught skepticism, even shame, for tribal ways, the African has learned to be equally skeptical of western beliefs and ways. He behaves as he does because of convenience or from expediency. Values disintegrate because the old values, which were not so very different from our own, were based on tribal lore that is now considered, by the sophisticated African, to be part of his regrettable savage past. The "new" values find no bedrock of belief on which they can establish themselves, and are not assumed with the rest of the trappings of western civilization. The result is a terrible degeneration, a lack of morality that was never known before. Vice of every kind is practiced without shame, because this is what the urban Africans have learned from their teachers.

Theft is an accepted corollary of urban life; prostitution, male and female, are accepted ways of earning a living; there is no shame in being the boy-lover or the mistress of a white man, rather it is a sign of success in this new world. The rural African coming into this kind of society may feel shame, but not those who are born into it. And even the rural African, if he stays long enough, loses his sense of shame because he quickly discovers that here he is no longer a member of a family, even of a tribe; that his neighbor is not bound by the same beliefs that bind him, and so can not be relied on to behave as a reasonable man. The only sensible and safe thing to do is to mistrust one's neighbor, to think for oneself alone, to have no consideration for others. This comes all the more easily because of the curious ways in which "national" boundaries were drawn by the colonial powers, and the resultant influx of people of many different tribes into any one urban center.

Nairobi may not be much more vice-ridden than any other large city, but vice is all the more noticeable there because of the sham respectability that hangs like a pall of white hypocrisy over its wide, clean avenues. The white community keeps its vice to itself in its segregated bars and hotels and clubs, and this induces an odd frustration in the African when a European decides to desegregate his vice life. It is easy enough to do so, and around Queen's Hotel you only have to look at one of the Africans, male or female, lounging around, to have them follow you and politely accost you in some secluded corner. This happened to me when I looked a little too hard at a remarkable African impersonation of a beatnik, leaning up against a parked car. He was about seventeen years old, dressed in jeans and an ill-fitting sweater. His hair had not been cut or combed for weeks by the look of it, and his pose was one of un-washed abandon. He returned stare for stare, then slowly ambled after me, keeping a respectful distance, stopping whenever I did, only coming closer when I finally sat down on a bench in an apparently unsegregated memorial garden.

William introduced his untidy self with great courtesy, and immediately asked me my name, nationality, place of birth and residence, and whether or not I was a missionary. He then asked me what I would like, saying he would be glad to get it for me. I said I was only staying a few days and wanted nothing in particular, at which he said he would give me a special low price and I could meet him after dark. If I had a car with a large back seat, that would be convenient, because he did not like taking white men to the native quarter of town, and presumably I would not want to take him to my room in the hotel. I agreed with him on the last two counts, and said I did not have a car. "Well, that's all right," he said "we can go over there." He indicated the center of the large parklike area, overgrown in places with tall grass and shrubs, interlaced with foul-smelling ditches of slimy black water. He continued to say that he would like to have given me a still better rate, as I was a stranger and not a missionary, but he had to go to court the next day and needed some money to pay a fine. He showed me the summons, assuming that I would not believe him.

William was a friendly soul, and was easily provoked into talking. He talked for about two hours, during which passers-by discreetly left us in seclusion. He said that he had been born in Nairobi, but that his parents had since gone back to the country. He spoke of them with scorn for being traditionalists, and used the Swahili word best translated as "savages." He said that they would have nothing to do with him because of the way he lived. "But what is wrong with it?" he asked. "It is what we all do, and it is expected of us. You taught it to us, so it must be good. All my friends here do the same thing—it gets very dull, but we make good money, and sometimes it is fun. But never with you English. You are so frigid, and all you ever want is a little excitement, usually when you are drunk, perhaps for a bet. When that happens we try to see to it that you get one of the boys with diseases. But some of the foreigners who come here to visit, they are much better. They are not so fussy, and they take us to their hotel or to their house and give us a good time as well as plenty of money. That is the other thing I can not understand about your people who live here. They live among us, they like to sleep with us, but they always seem so ashamed. Among each other they sleep freely with anyone they want to and even talk and joke about it, but they hide us as though we were something dirty. I had one like that last night. He owns a big farm at Naivasha, and he comes in to Nairobi every now and again to get away from his wife. I don't like him but he pays well and I have had him several times. But last night he was even more ridiculous than ever. We always arrange to meet after dark, because he doesn't like being seen talking to Africans, and yesterday he arranged to meet me at our usual spot by those bushes over there. He kept me waiting a long time, and I was annoyed with him, because I had other things to do. When he came he said he was in a hurry and we had to be quick. I took his money first, as I always do, and gave him what he wanted. It took me about thirty seconds. And before he had time to pull back his trousers I pushed him into the ditch and left him splashing in the dirt. I wonder how he explained that when he got back to his nice white hotel to change, because only Africans use that park."

William smiled with pleasure at the thought. Evidently the only reason he could see for the white settlers' showing such caution in their dealings with African boys and girls was because of their color; it had nothing to do with the immorality involved. William laughed outright at the latter thought. "Go to any of the bars," he told me, "and you can get whatever you want—white—for free. They would take you to their hotel, or to their home; they would walk around with you openly and show you off to all their friends. But for us it is the smelly park. Even the missionaries won't take us to their homes. That is why I never sleep with a missionary, because they say one thing with their mouths and do another with their bodies. We know the other white men don't like us. And I never take a white man to my home. They have made us live there, in those broken-down shacks, and they say, 'There, black man, that is your home—you live there and we shall live here, in the comfortable hotels and fine big houses.' So I think of my shack as being mine, and no white man or woman has ever set foot inside my door. I keep it clean."

Only at this point did William really seem bitter. For the rest of the two hours he talked openly and frankly. To him there was nothing abnormal about what he was doing, it was an accepted part of Nairobi life. The only emotions he had about it were his resentment of the settlers who insisted on clandestine meetings by night, lest they be accused of being "nigger lovers," and his consuming hatred of all missionaries. The latter hatred was almost matched by his hatred for traditionalists, including his parents. For William had been to the Mission School, and had been taught that his parents were savages. It was too late when he discovered that the missionaries also were savages.

As the street lamps came on he smiled hopefully and asked me again if he couldn't do anything for me, and reduced his price a further ten shillings. He even offered to get me a girl, though he did not seem to think that this was the right thing to do. . . . I said no, gave him his summons money, and embarrassed him by walking back toward the Queens Hotel with him.

William was a good, thoroughgoing atheist, consciously rejecting both tribal beliefs and the new, Christian beliefs, because he could not reconcile them with the reality of life. He lived a life that was amoral rather than immoral—in his world *morality* was another word for hypocrisy. But on the far side of Africa, in Accra, I met a young girl, in a similar profession to William's, but who seemed to be at least a nominal Christian, judging by the large crucifix hung around her pretty neck.

Ruth, like William, had absolutely no sense of shame. She did what was expected of her in the new world in which she had grown up. She lived with her parents, who were apparently completely uninterested so long as their daughter kept out of trouble and could afford to pay her share of the family expenses. But she did not have to face the same kind of frustrations as William, because in Accra relationships between white and black were almost completely free. Her profession did not demand of her the necessity for getting her clothes dirty in the middle of a clump of bushes. Whatever the color of her clients she could go with them freely to hotels, bars, night clubs or to their homes. Where William had been cynical, she was tolerant; where he was filled with hate, she was just simply not interested. The church she went to every Sunday was, admittedly, an all-African church, but she would not be turned out of the white church if she went there, she told me. When I asked her what the church thought about her professional activities she seemed surprised that I should see any connection. It had nothing to do with the church. "They accept my money," she said, "and they certainly know where it comes from. I am not doing anything wrong; I am not a thief, I don't steal married men away from their wives and make them live with me just because I have their children."

Ruth was in every sense a professional. She had thought a great deal about her work, she had some pride in it, and she had made some sacrifices for it. I used to see quite a lot of her because her headquarters was a bar where I used to like to drink and dance, and I came to know her reasonably well. She confessed that she had designs on me, because, she said, it would be so nice to be the mistress of a white man—provided he was not married. They are so rich. . . . I asked why did she not get married if she was so particular about bachelors. She was not so fond of her profession that she would not have been able to give it up. But somehow marriage did not enter into her scheme of things. Even in Accra marriage between white and black was not countenanced with equanimity by either side, but there was nothing wrong with a white man's having a black mistress. And as Ruth said, from the black girl's point of view every white man was rich.

Ruth visualized herself not as living in sin, but rather as living an honorable life with the man of her choice. She was very quick to point out that she had no use for the local brothels. They *were* sinful, she said. She spoke of them with real disgust, because there a girl does not have any choice in the matter, and what Ruth wanted, as well as money, was love. It was really very charming listening to this beautiful, mission-educated young girl talking with enthusiasm about her religion and all that it had to say about love and brotherhood, and equating those teachings with her life, justifying the one by the other with the logic of a grasshopper. Ruth was not one to parade in a brothel to be picked out by anyone that happened to like her looks. She was every bit a woman, and she chose her men—unless she needed money very badly and could not afford to be choosy.

I asked her if she had any children, and she said no, she had not been able to save enough yet. But she wanted children badly, white men's children, whether she was the mistress of their father or not. They were a completely separate need in her life, and they had to be part white, not for the financial reasons that to some extent, at least, ruled her heart, but because of the enormous prestige she envisaged. She saw herself sending her half-white children to school, taking them to church. She saw herself as the elderly mother of young mulatto men and women who themselves would have married either other mulattoes or full whites . . . as the grandmother of *nearly* pure whites. And this world of make-believe was filled with an undeniably real love. It was partly the mystical love and brotherhood that she heard so much about in church, but had met so little in practice, and it was partly her traditional need, as an African woman, for a family.

In contrast to William, there was no hate in Ruth's life. In Accra the two worlds had enjoyed a much longer time in which they were able to get used to each other's idiosyncrasies. In Ruth's church, for instance, drums were beaten and a mild form of dancing was permitted as an expression of religious fervor. The Mission School to which Ruth had gone as a child had baptized her at the age of fourteen or so, and then lost interest in her. Baptism seemed to be the graduation ceremony after which all connection was broken. The crucifix that Ruth wore was something in the nature of an old school tie. She had been taught how to read and write, she had been sprinkled with water as a symbol of her scholarly success, and that was all. Unlike William, she had not been weaned away from her parents, who were still not baptized, and she was not, again unlike William, ashamed of them. There was no difference between them, except in the status proudly proclaimed by the pendant hung around her neck. I tried to talk to Ruth about her church and her religion, but she was plainly bored. Church was a place to go to on Sunday because everyone did it. Church had nothing to do with the Mission, which was where children were taught to read and write, where you could occasionally get money or free medical treatment. And as for belief, what did I expect? Of course she believed, as she had always believed, that after death she would go to join her ancestors. What did all this have to do with whether or not she was to become my mistress?

When Ruth finally understood that I was leaving, and would not be able to take her with me, she was sorry. In a way so was I, because I think that as a mistress she would have been as faithful as any wife.

At Stanleyville, in the heart of the then Belgian Congo, a Protestant Mission was disinclined to have me as a visitor, paying or otherwise. It was even disinclined to discuss its work because I was the wrong kind of Protestant. But the Catholic Mission was most hospitable. They warned me, however, to keep everything locked up. My first day there a pen was stolen—it was not a particularly valuable one, but it had been a good friend and I was sorry to see it go. I did not bother to say anything, feeling that it was my own fault for having left it lying around.

A few days later I was sitting on the stone wall that runs along the riverside promenade, looking across the huge Congo river to the "native" town on the far side. There are ferries that run across almost continually, bringing workers to and from the city. I often used to sit there watching the ferryboat filling up with an overload of brightly clad, joking, jostling Africans, eager to get away from the white city and back to their own world on the far side of the river. There were native quarters on the outskirts of the city too, but they were drab and sordid, and much less full of life. Perhaps the villages on the distant shore were drab as well; I never went there, preferring to imagine that there was at least that one splash of brightness in the otherwise miserable surroundings. Even for the Europeans Stanleyville can hardly be said to be a beautiful city, and the few centers of entertainment that made it at all bearable were strictly reserved for whites. But across the water, gleaming in the whimsical light of the setting sun, the banks were green with grass and trees, and the boatloads of Africans going home after a day's work filled the river with song and laughter.

Usually I was ignored as the crowd surged toward the floating piers, carrying loads on their heads or bicycles on their shoulders, leaping down the steps and jumping onto a ferry as it pulled out, eager not to waste a precious minute in getting back to the world they knew and loved. But this particular evening a boy about fourteen years old came and sat down beside me, and by way of introduction handed me my pen. He said that his friend André had stolen it, but had been persuaded to give it back when he heard that I was a friend of Chief Kachui, of his tribe.

At first the boy, whose name was Antoine, made no apology, except insofar as I had been mistaken for an ordinary white man who did not have any African friends, and who was therefore fair game. He asked me about Kachui and about the people to the east of Stanleyville, and wistfully said that he wished he could travel but he spent all his life in the city, and with the high cost of living and the heavy taxes he was unable to save enough to go away. He then reverted to the matter of the theft and said that he hoped I did not mind, and that I would understand that André was a Christian . . . as though that might explain the whole thing. I assured him I did not mind in the least, and asked him if *he* was a Christian.

Antoine gave a vehement shake of his head and said certainly not, but he had been baptized and he worked at the Mission because he got a good education that way, was paid reasonably well and was not expected to work day and night. The only other possibility for him would have been a job as a houseboy, and he had too much pride for that. He went on to say that he would not steal himself, least of all from a guest, but the white men all stole from each other and from the Africans and many Africans followed their ways. "That is why I live with my parents over there," he said, pointing across the river. "We are not savages there, and we do not steal."

He went on to admit that occasionally he did take a little food from the Mission kitchen to bring home to his parents, because they were poor and they refused to come into Stanleyville to work. After all, the Mission had so much food and always taught that earthly possessions should be shared, so it was hardly stealing. "But if I was caught," he said, "I would first be beaten and then handed over to the police like a criminal. I have seen the reverend fathers stub their cigars out in the food left on their plates so we shall not be able to eat it or take it home. They are a heartless people, and think only of themselves. I shall never be a Christian." Little by little it came out, the enormous contempt that this fourteen-year-old boy had for the Mission, by whom he judged all Christians. It was not only that he had to suffer daily all manner of petty personal indignities, but the indignity foisted on his whole race by these "men of God" was reflected in his young mind.

"You have not been here on Sunday yet," he said. "When Sunday comes, go to Mass in the cathedral. There it is, right above us, looking across the river. You may find a few white men there, standing all by themselves. But go around the back, where the road faces into the white man's city, and see for yourself what sort of God these men serve. It is a lie; the whole thing. There is not a thing that they preach with their mouths which they believe with their minds and do with their bodies. Their whole life is a lie. Some of my friends here tell me it is part of a plan to keep us from learning the real truth, about them and their God, and I think this must be so. They do not want us to know their secret."

On Sunday I went to Mass in the main part of the cathedral,

cold and bare, and it was all-African, as Antoine had said it would be. Then I wandered around to the far side of the Mission where, directly behind the cathedral, there was a luxurious, carpeted chapel. The road outside was lined with motor cars, some of them with African chauffeurs idly at work with a polishing rag for want of anything better to do. Inside, the faithful were at their devotions, in the comfort and seclusion of their private chapel, uncontaminated by the presence of as much as an African acolyte. Later one of the priests blandly explained it to me. "Of course we don't believe in segregation, but the Africans smell, and while we priests are used to it the congregation is not. It would be terribly distracting to them. But of course if anyone *wants* to worship with the Africans he is welcome to come to our African services."

The funny thing is that many Africans think that Europeans are the ones who smell.

Across the forest, several hundred miles from Stanleyville, lies another town, Bukavu. This is a tourist resort, set on the shores of Lake Kivu in one of the most beautiful parts of all Africa. To the north two volcanoes light up the sky at night, and to the west the forest mountains rise steeply from the water's edge. Across the lake and to the south the country is open, the rolling hills green and lush, dotted with clumps of trees and interlaced with sparkling streams—this is the pleasant land of Ruanda Urundi, and Bukavu is just a mile or two on the Congo side of the border.

Bukavu itself is an attractive town with an air of a *Swiss* resort about it, and the elegance of its living is (or used to be) attested by the restaurants boasting famous Continental chefs. A good meal might cost twenty dollars, and the bill was brought to you by an imaginatively attired African waiter who was probably being paid between one and two dollars a week, and considered himself a millionaire because on top of that he might earn another dollar or two in tips. But generally gratuities went into a fund, and were redistributed by the manager, who deducted this and that for breakages, uniform, laundry, and an item conveniently labeled "incidental expenses." This was to pay police fines when workers had been kept working past curfew hours and were put in jail for the night on their way home.

I stayed at one of the fashionable hotels, on the shore of the lake, and found that by far the most agreeable soul there was the bartender, a short six-foot Tussi* named François Rwamashuli. François said that the only way he could get the benefit of my gratuities was by drinking them, and I used to stand guard while he hid beneath the bar and swallowed a glass of rum. Eventually he felt obliged to return some of these drinks, and invited me out for an evening on the town with other members of the hotel staff.

We drove in my car through the fashionable quarters of town, past all the night clubs and theaters, down by a little bay, and up into the native quarter. This may not have been as elegant as the rest of Bukavu, but it was certainly more lively. At about three in the morning we were all thrown out of a bar, or at least the others were thrown and I was more politely escorted, because of some altercation over my presence there. François and one of the others lived across the Congo-Ruanda border, up in the hills, and they asked me if I would mind driving them back, as otherwise they would have to spend the night in jail, not having a pass from the hotel. I drove them home, passing the border freely because of my color, and so began a long association with this Watussi family. The drive up the hillside was steep and rough, and I did not feel in any condition to return to Bukavu when I finally arrived at François' little house. He invited me in, had his wife make up a bed on the floor for me. He asked her sister to sleep with me to keep me warm, apologizing for the shortage of blankets.

The Tussi, or Watussi, are renowned for their great height. In fact it is only the Royal Family that are excessively tall; many of them are over seven feet.

I came to know François and his family well, and spent a great deal of time at their home high up in the hills of Ruanda. It took François two hours to walk to work every day, and two hours back at night. But it was worth it to him just to be rid of the town. Apart from the bars and the dancing in the native quarter of Bukavu there was nothing that François liked about the place. He liked the people still less. It was not so much the disparity of income that offended him, for he was content enough with his wages, but it was the attitude of the hotel owners that their staff should look as "native" as possible, in order to amuse the tourists. They were all forbidden to wear shoes, for one thing, and this upset François more than anything because he had been taught in the Mission School to dress correctly, and this was a direct blow at his pride. He was also indignant at the constant difficulty he had with the police at the border. When returning late at night he was meant to have a pass from the hotel manager, but often the manager was too drunk to sign it, or couldn't be bothered, or he was in bed with one of the guests. Then François would be arrested and would have to be bailed out the next day, his wages being duly docked.

Staying with François one weekend I realized just how deeply his pride was hurt. Up in the hills of Shangugu he was on his own land, master of his household, a man greatly respected by his neighbors because he was always willing to share his wealth. His wife was a beautiful Tussi girl, almost as tall as François, and the proud mother of a three-year-old son, Frederico. Their home was a simple one-room hut with a tin roof and mud walls, divided inside by a grass screen. To them it was a palace because it was theirs, as was the land on which it stood. The only sign of Western civilization was the road, a thousand feet below, winding along the valley floor towards a Catholic mission. The road up past their home was just a rough stone track, and François joked about preferring it like that because it stopped any whites from using it. "Otherwise they would come and stare at us like animals in the zoo," he said.

Even that small evidence of Western civilization François regretted. He talked continually of his mother's home, three days' walk away across the hills, where there were no roads and no missions. But he felt he could no longer live there. He had received a good education at the Mission School, and had learned many things. He thought the new way of life was good, and it would obviously be wonderful to be able to live like the white men, in big houses, with cars, and pay two months' wages for a single meal, or a week's wages for a drink. The Mission where he had been educated had been kind to him, and had taught him well. He thought that the doctrine of love was a wonderful thing and was glad that the white man had brought an end to the fighting between his people and the other tribes. Now they were all friends, and could eat and drink together as they had been taught to at the Mission. It was only with the white man that you could not be friends, only with him that you could not eat and drink . . . even in church.

He did not entirely blame the church for this. He thought of it as some political maneuver that was forced on the church by the government to maintain white supremacy. The church said it would like to see an end to all these petty differences. The only thing that François did blame the church for was the enigma of segregated Communion. If the bread and the wine were really the flesh and blood of Christ, he asked, were they not more powerful than the white man's laws that segregated white from black? Or did the white man really think that the African was so dirty that even the flesh and blood of Christ would be contaminated? It was something that he could not understand, so he no longer went to church. He still retained his faith in the new way of life, but at the same time he kept himself and his family as far away from it as possible.

One Sunday morning we sat in the little garden outside his home, and looked down into the valley below. There was a long line going down the hillside toward the Mission; the women clad in flowing yellow and white robes, and the men dressed, as François always was, in neat white suits. François said that a number of them worked for the Mission, and were even better paid than he was. "But what is the good?" he asked. "Their bellies are full and their hearts are empty." A short distance away, not far from the border post, a market was being held. Canoes came across the lake, laden with bananas and other foods. We could see the crowd milling about, men and women half naked as they sweated under their loads in the sun while the seemingly endless procession of church-goers continued to amble by.

"If only the Christians and the white men could be like them," murmured François, "and have their hearts as full of love as their mouths; and if only they could be like the Christians, and wear proper clothes."

8

Ibrahimo

"I do not think my father was a Christian when he married my mother; I know they married in the way of our own people anyway. But he became a Christian before I entered my mother's stomach, and took the name Isaaka. So when I was born and had shown that I had come to this world to stay he called me Ibrahimo, because it is our custom to name our children after their grandfathers. I do not know what my grandfather's name really was, my father never speaks of him.

By becoming a Christian my father won a good job as a cook at the Mission. He had to leave because my mother refused to change her ways, and the Mission would not have her there living with him, because they said they were not married. So they returned to Ndola and I was born here and have lived here ever since. There are other Christians at Ndola, but my father has told me that the Mission does not want us to have anything to do with them, they do not believe in the same God. Their leader uses his *baraza* as a church, and has services every Sunday, but we never go, it would be a sin. My father did not like me to play with their children, so at Ndola I have no Christian friends. But I used to have plenty of other friends, and my mother was always very good to us and gave us plenty of good things to eat when we were hungry.

As I grew older my father said I should not play even with my own brothers, and that I should go away to school, to the Mission on the far side of Matidi. My mother did not like this, and there was much fighting and beating. In the end, my mother left my father, and while she was away I was taken to school.

It was a good place, though all the buildings were made of brick and were hot, unlike the houses we build. And we were not allowed to light fires inside at night, to keep us safe and to keep the mosquitoes away. Even if we could have lit them it would not have done much good as every wall was broken open with windows, and the smoke would all have escaped. But we learned many things, how to read and write and how to play the strange games of the white man with leather balls. This hurt my feet terribly at first, for we were not allowed to wear shoes, although nearly all of us had them. They said it would spoil the shoes.

I heard that when Bwana Lewis was there the houses were like ours, made of mud and thatched with leaves, and that there were some trees left to give shade, but as soon as he left Bwana Spence cut down all the trees and built the brick houses. But he also made a big kitchen and fed all the people who worked for him, and all the children at the school. That is why so many come here. Only a few bring their own food because they do not trust food cooked by strangers. They are not real Christians.

But it was difficult to know how to be a Christian, because Bwana Spence did not like to be asked questions. He read to us from the Big Book and often it did not make sense. When I was still new there I would ask questions, and sometimes he would answer them, but usually he said I did not have to understand, I just had to believe what he said. He got very angry if we asked about all the men in the Big Book who had so many wives, when he taught us that when we were older we should have only one. He said that Bwana Yesu said so. But neither Bwana Yesu nor any of his brothers had any wives, so how could they know?

He also did not like us to talk to the girls. We were taught separately, and we lived in separate buildings—those of us who came from far away. Now, it is obviously a bad thing for a boy not to know a girl, and we used to visit each other's houses. Amboko told us it was all right because really they were just like our bachelor houses, it was simply that Bwana Spence had not married until late and did not understand these things. When Bwana Spence had first come to our land he was already a man, but had no wife, and this was not good. He used to look at the women, Amboko said, but never knew them. If they spoke to him he was afraid and ran away. So we understood that there must have been something wrong with Bwana Spence when he was a boy and he did not learn how one should behave. This was one of the things he would never explain to us, merely telling us to do as he said. So we only met the girls at night, when he could not see us and would not be offended.

But there were some things that could not be just because Bwana Spence did not understand. In his teachings he told us to be like brothers to each other, to share everything we had and to help each other. But while there were many of us in one house, sleeping in the same room even though we were from different tribes, he had a house all to himself. He ate three big meals a day while we had two, and his food was much better and much more plentiful. He bought all manner of things at Matadi to eat himself, and we never tasted any of it. He had lots of clothes, and he had many servants to wait on him and do all his work for him. He never asked us into his house, although he would come to ours. In the evenings even if his wife was at the hospital and he was alone he would not talk to any of us, but just stayed by himself, eating, and drinking his tea or coffee. He was never without food, day or night. He must have been very wealthy.

He had a child too, a girl child who had not yet seen the blood, but he would not let her play with any of us or even talk to us. There were some other white children at the Mission but they all lived in the white man's houses, and were taught separately and ate separately and played separately. It was a pity. They could have had a lot of happiness with us.

Bwana Spence's wife was a proud woman who did not smile. She gave orders, even to men, and got very angry when anyone disobeyed her. She taught the white children, and she worked at the hospital. She always looked as though she was going to be sick, although when I asked her once if she was not well she said she was perfectly all right. She lied. She was not all right. A relative of mine came to the hospital while I was there because her stomach was full and hurting, but the child would not come. She had been bound with vines and had tried everything she knew to make the child come, but it refused. When Bwana Spence's wife saw her she told her that the child had not wanted to come because it had been put into the stomach in sin. It could still be saved, she said, if my relative would become a Christian and have a Christian marriage. But my relative was already married, and said she could not be married again. I think the Bwana Spence's wife put a curse on her, because the first part of the child to come out was a hand, and the rest of it was dead. They say that this was one time when Bwana Spence's wife smiled.

We were allowed to go home during holidays, but I liked it at the school because I had many friends there, and at Ndola the people thought of me as being different, like my father, and they laughed at me. But the longer I stayed at the Mission the more I was worried. They were doing very good things for us, but they did not seem to like us or want us to be their friends. They were very selfish about their God too, and although they used to ask Him, when we all talked to Him together, to look after us and save our souls and accept us as His children, they never let *us* stand up and ask for things. They would ask for new motor cars or for money to make roads so that they could travel farther and meet more of our people and make them Christians, but they never let *us* ask for motor cars.

And once when Bwana Spence's girl child was hot with fever he made us all ask together for her to be made better, though none of us had even spoken to her. We thought this funny, because she had been hot with fever before, as we all were at times, and it was nothing serious. But we asked for her to be made better, and two days later she was. But that same week a man was brought in who was very ill indeed, and Bwana Spence did not even go to see him, and did not ask God to help him, because, he said, the man was not a Christian. We all thought this was a terrible thing, and we wondered and talked among ourselves about what kind of God this was. We knew we could not ask Bwana Spence, so we asked Amboko. Amboko was almost as cross with us as Bwana Spence would have been, for the man was his relation. I think he was cross because he could not explain it either. I began to wonder if I would be allowed to ask God to help my mother if she became ill, because she is not a Christian. Amboko said no, I would have to ask the ancestors, that they would always listen.

I had been at the school perhaps two years when something very bad happened. I was home on vacation and one day Matungi came up to me and took me into the plantation to talk with me. This was a great honor, for Matungi is really our chief, and he is a great and good man. I think I knew what he wanted, though, and I was afraid. It had been three years since the last *nkumbi* initiation festival, and it was time for another. At this festival we boys are taken and we are made into men. It is a very difficult and dangerous thing, and I do not know much about it except that our foreskins are taken away from us to make us clean, and we are given the marks on our bodies that make us acceptable to the ancestors. These festivals used to last many months, even a year, but now the Bwana Mkubwa at Matadi does not like it because he says it takes us all away from our work, and the white Christians all say it is evil. They do not know, because they do not understand and are as ignorant about it as little children.

Matungi told me that it was time for me to enter the *nkumbi*, and to learn the ways of my ancestors. He said that he did not mind me learning to read and write, or even being a Christian, but that it was very wrong for me to forget who I was. He said that only by seeing the *nkumbi* could I make myself fit for the ancestors; by becoming like them I could become one of them. This was plainly a good thing, and Matungi further showed me that no matter what the Christians said, nobody could deny that I had a father, and he had a father, and his father before him had a father. Nobody could deny that we did have ancestors, and if we had ancestors how could it be right to neglect and disrespect them when they made life possible for us? I told Matungi that even the Christian teachings said the same thing, and told us that we were to honor our fathers and mothers.

Matungi was very wise, and I told him that although I was frightened, I *did* want to see the *nkumbi*. He was very pleased, and he gave me a cigarette and told me that I would soon be a real man, and that I would be glad. He also told me not to be frightened, that only children were frightened.

I ran straight back through the plantation to the village and told my brothers. They were all very surprised, and they congratulated me and said they were happy, because they had been afraid that I would be separated from them and not become a man with them. Now we would all do this dangerous thing together and become men together, and we would all learn the wonderful secrets about our ancestors, and learn how to please them and earn a place beside them in the afterworld. We celebrated by running after some girls and chasing them into the plantation and playing with them. It was the first time I had really ever played with my brothers. I was very happy, and very proud. When we had finished playing I went to my mother's plantation and told her. I thought she would be pleased, although I expected her to wail because women always wail at this time, for they are losing their children. They would not have it otherwise, though, because they too are proud and want their boys to be men. My mother did not wail. She looked frightened and put her arms around me as though I were a suckling infant still drinking her milk. She held me close to her breasts so that I could feel their warmth flowing into me. She told me that my father might not like it, and that I had better sleep that night with my brothers, and come to her the next morning. She asked me if I knew that I was a Christian, and that Christians do not see the *nkumbi*. But I told her that my father had seen it, so surely he would want me to. After all, even white Christians must have ancestors. She said it was a big matter, and she would have to talk to my father, and she would get Matungi to talk to him. She said that she hoped I would never forget my ancestors, and she pushed me away. When I left, I think she was crying.

But I was sure my father would want me to do as he had done, because we had the same grandfather and nearly all the men of our village were of the same family. I spent the night with my brothers and told them all about the strange ways of the white man at the Mission School, how some things were good and others bad. They laughed when I told them about the way they tried to keep the boys away from the girls, and how we tricked them because we knew better. They said we had done right, because look what had happened to Masoudi, our capita, and how everyone laughed at him for a fool and simpleton even though he had found a wife in the end.

Late that night there was a big noise in the village, and I was frightened again. But I hid it, and said nothing. I was sorry, because I had wanted it to be a good night—it was the first time I had ever slept with my brothers. I dreamed of all the wonderful times to come, and of all the friends I would have from now on. Early in the morning I hurried out to my mother's plantation, but she was not there. I went home, and she was not there, neither was my father. This was not strange, as everyone goes about his work in the morning, so I went back to the plantation to wait for my mother. She did not come.

At last, when my stomach was crying for food, my father came, calling my name. I ran up to him and waited for him to speak, but he hit me on the back with his fist and said I had done a terrible thing. He had worked hard to send me to the Mission School, and he had sent me a little money each month so that I could buy things I needed, and now I wanted to throw it all away by seeing the *nkumbi*. He took me back to the house and locked me in, throwing me a little food that had been left over from the morning. It was cold and I could not eat it. I called for my mother, but she did not answer. I didn't know how many days I was kept there; I only remember thinking that I must truly still be a child because I cried so much, but I could not help it.

What followed is so bad that I try to forget it, and I do not like to talk about it. One morning the Bwana Spence's motor car came and I was put into it and driven away. I still had not seen my mother, and although I saw Matungi and called to him from the window he just turned away. If I had been a man I would have jumped out, but I could not. I was sick. I was still being sick when we reached the Mission, and I no longer had the strength to lean out of the window. I was sick all over the back of the car. When Bwana Spence saw this he was more angry than I had ever seen him. He had me taken away to the hospital, to cure my sickness.

He came to see me later, and I told him that I wanted to see the *nkumbi* just as my father had seen it, that only in that way could I be a man. I told him all that Matungi had said, and he replied that Matungi was evil, and when he died would go to the fires that never go out. I told him about my brothers, and how they were all glad that I was joining them, and how it was the first time I had really played with them. Bwana Spence asked me if I did not have enough friends at the Mission, and I said yes, but they were not my brothers—I wanted to be friends with *them,* and to see the *nkumbi* with them and to share their blood, so that we could all live together as men-brothers, and go to the ancestors together. He told me that there was only one ancestor, and that was Bwana Yesu. I said that could not be, because Bwana Yesu was not married and did not have any children. I also told him that I thought Bwana Yesu was a lie invented to make us go to the white man's after-world and be his servants there. I do not know what made me say this thing, because I *did* believe in Bwana Yesu; but I said it, and Bwana Spence said that I was also evil, but that it was Matungi's fault and not mine. He said he would ask Bwana Yesu to forgive me, and that he would not let me go home again for any more holidays, I could stay at the Mission and help keep the place clean. He stood at the end of my bed and asked Bwana Yesu to forgive me and to make me a good Christian again, then he left. As soon as he left I asked Bwana Yesu to forgive me and to let me see the *nkumbi,* but I knew in my heart that he would listen to Bwana Spence and not me.

The next day I was no longer sick, but they still would not let me out of the hospital. They said I was not there because I had been sick but for another reason, and I did not understand what they meant. They came in and took hold of me and made me walk into a special house they have where they bring people who are dying, and cut them open. I was very frightened and tried to break away, because I knew I was not dying and they had told me I was not even sick. I thought that Bwana Spence was so angry at me for making his car dirty that he was going to kill me. He was there, in the house, and he smiled at me and said not to be frightened, that he had asked Bwana Yesu to stay with me, and that Bwana Yesu had told him how I wanted to be a man like other men, and had made him understand that this was right. At first I thought he meant that I was going to be allowed to return home to the *nkumbi,* but he said no, and told me to lie on the table. Only then did I begin to understand. I fought as hard as I could, but I could not get away. I remember Bwana Spence leaning on my arms, holding me down, and smiling. But there was no love in his smile, only hate. Then someone put something over my face. It smelled of vomit and I thought I was being sick again. I felt all my life being taken away from me, and I was sure I was dying. The last thing I remember is Bwana Spence smiling. And then I died.

When I woke up I had no feeling. I knew there was a terrible pain in my body, but my mind was empty, and I just did not care about the pain. All I wanted was to *feel* again, to feel as though I was alive. But I could not. I saw the wife of Bwana Spence standing over me, but when she saw I recognized her she turned away. I saw other people, but they did not mean anything to me. I heard noises, but I just wanted them to stop because they were empty noises. And then I knew I was dead. I knew it because the pain got worse, and as it got worse it no longer came from my whole body, it came from one place, the place where they had cut me with their knives. I could not see the cut, I could not see the blood, because I was covered with a sheet and I had no strength to move my hands to find what they had done. But I knew, because the pain came from my penis, where they had cut off my skin so that I would never be able to see the *nkumbi,* and would never be able to be a man. I remember crying out loud—not because of the pain, but because of what they had done to me, and I was sick again.

When my body got better I found that Bwana Spence had gone back to where he had been living for some time with his wife, near Ndola. This was a good thing, because there was much hate in my heart for what he had done, and I knew now that he hated me. Amboko was with him too, so I was alone, and I was too ashamed to talk of this thing with the other children. After a while I could not stand it, and I escaped and walked all the way home. I arrived at night so that I would not be seen, and went to my father's house. Nobody was there, so I went in and lay down and went to sleep.

Later that night I woke up and saw my father sitting on a chair in the doorway. He knew I was there because when I called to him he was not surprised. I asked him where my mother was, and he said she had left him and gone away. Then I saw that there was someone else in the room, and I knew that my father had taken another wife. I asked him how he could do this when it was against the teachings of Bwana Yesu, the same teachings that had made him stop me from seeing the *nkumbi*. He was silent for a while, then he told me he did not know what he was doing, and he asked me to question him no further. He said there were many things we would have to talk about, and that he was glad I had come home. He knew what had happened to me, and he told me that in his eyes, anyway, I was a man. This made me happy, and I slept well.

Those were difficult days for me, because my brothers made fun of me for not having joined them. They asked me why I walked awkwardly, as if I had been cut, and they laughed. I told them that I had been with a girl and had caught the white man's disease, which had made my penis swell, but they did not believe me. I think they were sorry for me because although they made fun of me, they were kind, but I knew that we could never really be friends now, and never share our blood. One of them told me that after I had been locked up in my father's house my mother had left and gone away to her own village because of the great evil her husband had done, and that shortly afterwards my father had been bewitched by this other woman into taking her as wife. He had given many goats and much wealth, more than he had given when he married my mother. But although she had bewitched him, I was told, she was a good woman, it had not been her fault. I did not understand them. I was also told that Amboko had had a big fight with Bwana Spence, and that Bwana Spence was going back to Matadi in a great rage. I did not understand that either, because Amboko had been a good friend to the Bwana Spence always, and had suffered much ridicule as a result.

But a few days later my father called me to drink beer with him. I was proud, although we were alone and there were no other men with us, because we sat out in front of our house, like men, for all the village to see. His wife brought us the beer and we drank in silence. Then he told me. He said he had done what he had done because he felt that our world somehow now belonged to the white man. He did not know how this had come about, but it was so. And the only way to be a man in this new world, he thought, was to be a Christian. There were many good things in the teachings of Bwana Yesu, and they were not unlike our own teachings. And we were taught to call him "Father," so perhaps he was an even greater ancestor, further back than we had ever thought of, ancestor of black and white alike. This is how my father once believed, how he still believed when he sent for Bwana Spence to take me away so that I would not be forced to enter the *nkumbi*. My father said he did not know that Bwana Spence was going to circumcise me, but I think his heart knew it. Anyway it was done.

After the news reached Ndola that I had been cut in the hospital, and had not even suffered it like a man but had been asleep, someone put a terrible curse on my father and caused him to become bewitched so that now he had not only transgressed against our ancestors, he had also transgressed against the white man's ancestors. And he knew that they were different ancestors now, that Bwana Yesu was not really our "Father," because of a dream he had had. In this dream Bwana Yesu had appeared to him. It was the first time he had seen Bwana Yesu, except in photographs, and he looked very closely. Bwana Yesu was white, and all his children around him were white. Bwana Yesu pointed to the children and told my father that unless he changed and became like that child he could not enter the Kingdom of the Clouds.

I told my father that I had heard Bwana Spence tell the same story, but he had never explained it except by saying that we must remain as children. My father said that this was what worried him so, because what it obviously meant was that Bwana Yesu was white, and that only uncircumcised white people could enter the

Kingdom of the Clouds. Bwana Spence had circumcised me so that I would not be able to enter his kingdom or that of my ancestors. I asked then, in surprise, if Bwana Spence was not circumcised, and my father told me about Amboko, and why he had left. Bwana Spence had discovered that his Bwana had never been cut and was unclean.

My father went on to say that Bwana Yesu had added a powerful curse that anyone who harmed one of his children would be drowned in the river. This proved beyond doubt that I was not his child, even though I had been baptized and called Ibrahimo, because otherwise Bwana Spence would not have dared to harm me. I remembered the look on Bwana Spence's face, and at last I understood.

I learned how Bwana Spence had fought with Matungi, and had called him evil, and had cursed him and told him he would never die but would live on forever like a ghost in a terrible world of flames. I learned how he had caused Matungi to be ridiculed and insulted by the administrator at Matadi, and how only the ancestors had saved Matungi from being put away in a box. I saw that my father had no bitterness against Matungi for the curse; for although he was sorry to lose his first wife, my mother, he had been forced by Matungi to give up his mistaken beliefs and come back to the ways of the ancestors. And after a while my mother would come back to him, and he would be blessed with two wives.

I was glad for my father, but for myself I now knew that I had truly died when they brought me into that house of the knife. I knew why Bwana Spence had not wanted to explain things, but tried to make us believe that the words of Bwana Yesu were good words and would help us to be good people. I knew now that his Bwana's kingdom really was in the clouds, although he said it was not, and that it was quite different from ours that is in the earth. I knew that in order to go to Bwana Yesu's kingdom I had to be white and uncircumcised, and that I could be neither. I also knew that my ancestors would not want me because I had not seen the *nkumbi*.

I went to see Matungi, and he tried to make me strong. He said that even he did not understand all these matters. He had always thought that Bwana Yesu was a good man, and it was the Bwana Spence who was lying, because he knew of other white men who *were* circumcised. I asked him if he meant Bwana Banduki, the white man who was circumcised by the Bafwamiti and who worked growing strange plants and fruits for the administrator. But Matungi said no, that even Christian white men circumcise each other.

Then I began to hate Bwana Spence because of all his lies, and because of all the unhappiness he had brought to my father and to Matungi and to myself. I felt he was the most evil thing I had ever met, and I asked Matungi to perform a special rite to make both my father and myself clean again in the eyes of our ancestors. But Matungi said he could do it for my father, but that I had not seen the *nkumbi,* and he did not know what he could do for me. He said that the ancestors were able to understand these things, and he would ask them to look after me, and maybe they would talk to him in a dream and tell him what to do.

Meanwhile he told me that he thought the best thing was for me to go back to the Mission School and to continue with my learning. They would have to take me back after what they had done, he said. Matungi warned me to have nothing to do with Bwana Spence, not to trust a single white man there, not to believe a word they spoke, and never to join them in their ritual eating and drinking, because this might offend the ancestors even more. 'But,' he said, 'learn all you can. See for yourself if what Bwana Yesu says is the same thing as what the Bwana Spence says. You have been made one of Bwana Yesu's children by the water ceremony, and after all your father did not see in his dream whether the other children were circumcised or not. He thought they were too young—but maybe the Christians circumcise earlier than we do—and maybe Bwana Spence has an evil spirit in his body that makes him do and say these terrible things. If all that is so, and if you still believe in Bwana Yesu, you may go to his afterworld. You can not come to ours without seeing the *nkumbi.*'

All this Matungi told me, and my father said that Matungi had spoken well. We would have to accept it that in the afterlife we would be separated forever, for my father had decided to go back to the ways of his ancestors.

I went back to the school, and I am still there. I have learned a great deal, and I can now read the Big Book myself. But it does not always make sense, and it speaks of many things of which I still know nothing, and it is all about faraway places and about white men that can have nothing to do with me. I try to talk to Bwana Yesu but he does not talk back to me. I stop my ears when I hear Bwana Spence talking, because I do not want to be tricked by his lies. I look in his face and I know he is lying, and that he hates all of us. Even the young children know this and they laugh at him. I once thought of having a child by his daughter, thinking that in this way I might have access to the white man's afterworld, but Matungi told me this would be a very bad thing.

I do not know what will happen. I am told that the white man is soon going to leave, and then my learning will be useful. But for what? What good is learning if I can not marry a white girl and if none of our own girl-children will have me? If I can not in any way make myself clean and acceptable in this world, how can I be fit for life in the afterworld?

I met some BaNgwana the other day, and they told me that they have a god who will accept me and take me into his afterworld if I do certain things. But they are unclean things, and we all know the BaNgwana to be an unclean people. Perhaps I shall have no after-life, and in that case I can only do what I can with this life. And in this life I shall never believe a white man again. If I follow his ways it is with my body, not with my heart. In my heart there is only the knowledge that the white man has taken me away from my fathers and brothers for all time, and that he hates me. In that knowledge I can only find strength to hate back."

9

The Meeting
of the Two Worlds

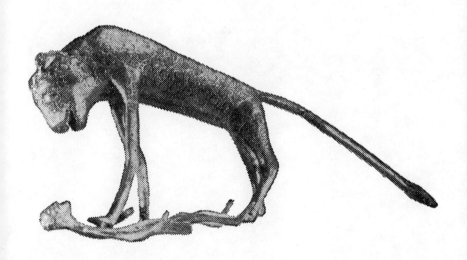

So far all we have seen has been conflict: a conflict of ideals, of personalities, of different ways of living and of understanding. This has been neither intentional nor unrepresentative; it has merely presented the situation as it is. But at the same time, the two worlds *have* met, whether we like it or not, and it is reasonable to suppose that there are instances where the meeting has been successful. Because such instances are rare and less obvious, they are nonetheless important. But exactly what do we mean by successful contact in this clash of civilizations?

A great deal of the present conflict arises because one side or the other sees in the situation a battle to the death, the only result of which can be complete victory for one side or the other. This is the stand commonly taken by the white settlers in East, Central and South Africa, and consequently many Africans in the same areas take a similar stand in self-defense. Where colonialism has been most aggressive, there you have the most violent antiwhite nationalism. But victory of the one group over the other can not solve the basic conflict unless the victory is accompanied by extermination or expulsion. It is still by no means impossible that this may be the ultimate solution.

In other parts of Africa, however, particularly on the west coast, feelings run much less high and while the Africans have seen more direct benefits from the presence of white civilization, the Europeans, by virtue of their political, economic and domestic status, have not had to rely on a policy of subjection. Here at least we might look for some meeting of the two worlds that has found a form of success that does not mean victory for the one and annihilation for the other.

We have seen something of the superficiality of acculturation in both urban and rural areas; for example, the superficiality of the African Christian who merely adopts the religion as part of his new cultural costume. We have seen the impossibility of the position the extremists attempt to hold, always falling ultimately into compromise or self-deception. It is impractical to be a traditionalist in a world changing as rapidly as Africa is changing, but it is equally impractical to adopt a totally new and different way of life without the kind of faith and belief that can come only with centuries of experience.

Intermarriage between peoples of the two races is one obvious example of how union may be achieved, at least at a personal level, and with a success that does not mean complete assimilation or obliteration for one side or the other—success not merely in that the married couples stay married and rear healthy families, but success in the sense of the achievement of spiritual union as well as a physical and cultural union. While intermarriage can not be advocated as a practical solution to the problem of how the two worlds are to learn to live together it does at least provide an example of how individuals manage to succeed where nations fail.

Interracial marriage is something that arouses the strongest emotion in many people, who often express their feeling as one of physical revulsion. Sometimes these people have the same revulsion at the thought of even touching a dark skin. This may be a neurosis, but it is nonetheless a fact, and a difficult one to counter, for it is beyond the realm of reason. Other opponents of intermarriage put forward many arguments in the attempt to be rational; sometimes they are pseudobiological, sometimes sociological. Frequently they are concerned with maintaining "racial purity" and they talk in terms that remind one of the fanatical racism of the Nazis.

It is as well, then, to state at the outset that generally accepted scientific inquiry has found no known grounds for assuming that there are any biological factors that militate against interracial marriage. On the contrary, any widening of the marriage circles to which we habitually confine ourselves, for one reason or another, has the considerable advantage of making less likely the sudden appearance of hidden recessive genes. Insofar as various races, by which we really mean biological subspecies within the single species of Homo sapiens, acquire distinctive characteristics by adaptation to distinctive environments, it might be argued that intermarriage will destroy that adaptive value. This is of no great concern, however, as such intermarriage is only likely to occur where man has learned to control the environment to a considerable degree. Various races acquired their characteristics due to geographic isolation which prevented the free circulation of genes, and it is only reasonable that with the removal of these geographic barriers through modern techniques of transportation, genetic circulation should be increased and racial differences become less prominent. This process has already gone far enough to make the existence of a "pure" race an extreme rarity, with little chance of prolonged survival.

While we can say with complete certainty that there are no demonstrable arguments against intermarriage, our knowledge of genetics is still incomplete and new facts may come to light at any time which may show that biological arguments *are* involved, either against or for. Instances of exceptional offspring from such a union, either children who are congenital idiots or who have abnormally high I.Q.'s, are often quoted, but these are isolated examples and the abnormalities are due to other factors than race—the same factors that can produce the same results within any single human group, however isolated or "pure."

There are, however, very strong sociological arguments that

should be taken into account, though they do not constitute in themselves a case against intermarriage as such. Under certain conditions the chances of success for such a marriage would be slight. In South Africa, for instance, even if it were legally possible, it would be *practically* impossible for white to marry black. The white come under one set of laws and live in one restricted area, black come under another set of laws and live in a different restricted area, and the offspring, who would be termed "colored," would come under a third set of laws and also be segregated. Though not codified in exactly this way, the same situation exists in East and Central Africa, as it does in many parts of the western world.

If we are to think in terms of sociological considerations we should be consistent and realize that the term *race* has now lost its biological connotations, and that we now think more in terms of nationality or culture. Many East African settlers who consider themselves liberal and enlightened strongly deny that they have any color bar. "It is a *culture* bar," they say. In fact it is anything but that, and it is the British of East and Central Africa who have done more than anyone to create the impression among Africans that the white man is, by nature, a hypocrite. But if it *were* a culture bar, it would be a considerable step forward to a solution of the conflict. Understood in this way the problem is similar to problems faced in our own home towns, wherever they may be, almost every day. There are many English families who would be horrified at the thought of their children marrying Germans. There are Scots who would feel shame if one of their kin married a Sassenach from south of the border. There are northern Italians who despise the southerners, and there are those in the southern states of America who would disapprove strongly of any marriage with a northern family. At an even more localized level there are strong feelings between aristocratic, professional, trade and artisan classes. All these feelings, with which we are familiar within our own "race," are the same feelings that we carry into the question of interracial marriage. Many of the motivations are similar, if not the same: political and economic considerations and concern for social status are dominant—and these are *real* considerations, unlike the imaginary biological arguments.

Once this is understood many of the deeply felt personal emotions fade away, though it takes time. Then we can see quite clearly why the situation can be so different in different parts of Africa. In the French-speaking West African territories, for instance, there is little personal feeling one way or the other. The French settlers and administrators have seen that their economic future and success is inextricably bound up with that of the African, so there is no great spirit of economic rivalry. In most of their former colonies the French are still there in their original capacities as administrators, planters, teachers, or as experts in the various scientific fields.

Not having felt any great rivalry with the African in either the political or economic field, the Frenchman feels little or no hostility toward him. This influences his attitude in the social realm, and there is consequently no stigma attached to intermarriage on purely racial grounds. A scientist with an illiterate girl from the bush for wife might be laughed at as an oddity, and considered a romantic, but he would not be attacked so long as he respected her as his wife and treated her as such. But elsewhere in Africa it would be impossible to respect an African girl as a wife and treat her as such. While throughout West Africa you are likely to find mixed couples anywhere, in the towns or out in the country, in East and Central Africa you would find at most a rare European with an African mistress, and even then only in the depths of the country. He might boast of it to a few friends but it would be something to hide from the general public, something that would bring him into scorn and contempt.

But we are talking here about marriages that are full and complete, in which children are reared as members of the family, not given away for some distant black relative to raise. On the whole such marriages are probably more frequent in urban areas than in the country, even in West Africa, and this is because in urban areas both races have a greater similarity of background. In the large West African cities the educational opportunities for Africans are much greater than elsewhere and this makes for much greater compatability, just as it does in our own society. There are still serious practical difficulties. There is always some feeling of hostility arising from national or family pride, and though this may come from outside the families concerned, it still makes itself felt. The mixed couple may be strong enough to withstand its effect, but for their children it is less easy. Fortunately this has not so far arisen as a major problem in Africa because the feeling of hostility on the African side is much less than it can be on the European side. A mixed marriage that would be a complete failure due to social pressures in some European or American towns can be a complete success in West Africa. But there is no doubt that in West Africa as elsewhere it helps if the parents have two assets: wealth and status.

Even then there are considerations that come into play that lessen the chances of success. Such was the case when Chief Seretse Khama married a London typist, Ruth Williams. The fact that Ruth was a typist should not have been of any great consequence, but it was. And in this case, although her husband had both wealth and status to make up for her lack, his particular status, instead of helping matters, only made them worse. He was chief of the Bamangwato tribe, in the British protectorate of Bechuanaland, an isolated semi-independent territory surrounded by the overtly racist territories of South Africa, Southern Rhodesia and Angola. Further, South Africa at that time was pressing its claims to ultimate control of this and two similar protectorates.

In England opinion was unfavorably swayed by the fact that Ruth was a mere typist. It was undignified and improper for royalty, even black royalty, to marry a commoner, and there was not even anything particularly romantic or exciting about Ruth's background to enhance her commoner's status. Had she been a chorus girl at the Windmill Theatre she would have had more status than she did as a typist. This was cunningly played up by the Europeans in Africa who told the Bamangwato that their chief was marrying below his station.

As for Seretse, the fact that he was chief carried little weight, for the power rested ultimately in the hands of the British High Commissioner, and even beyond *him* in the Houses of Parliament at Westminster. And Parliament had other things to worry about than the matrimonial prospects of Seretse and Ruth. They were more concerned with the violent reaction in South Africa to the mere possibility that the British government should allow such a union, particularly when a chief was involved, in a protectorate surrounded by rigidly enforced policies of apartheid. A number of threats were bandied back and forth, in the middle of which Seretse and Ruth, not without some ecclesiastical objections, were quietly married in the hopes that this would settle matters. But it did not. The question was now whether or not he should be deposed. The English administration in Bechuanaland called for the opinion of the Bamangwato themselves, and this seemed fair, although white propaganda was spread asking the people how they would like a half-caste as their next chief. Seretse campaigned more honestly and wisely, using Ruth herself as his argument. Ruth is a charming woman, and full of a natural dignity that made her quite equal to the occasion. The opinion of the Bamangwato, who were more concerned about Ruth as a woman than about her position in London society, was quietly won over to Seretse's side, and she quickly became a popular and much loved figure. This might have silenced some of the English critics, but it did not silence South African opinion, nor did it allay the fears of the British Parliament as to what action the South African Government might take. The status of the whole protectorate was a delicate political issue, and Seretse's marriage made it all the more so. It was unfortunate for Parliament that the invited opinion of the Bamangwato people themselves should have been in favor of their chief and his wife. The only thing to do was to ignore it.

Seretse was given to understand that all was well, and he told me that he firmly believed that the High Commissioner himself had this understanding from the home government. Seretse returned to England, at the request of the government, to settle his affairs, and promptly found himself exiled and separated from his wife, whom he had left in Bechuanaland. Public opinion almost reversed itself at this piece of diplomatic chicanery, though it was typical enough of colonial politics, but to no avail. Seretse was maintained in exile, deposed, and his wife was thoughtfully flown back to him at government expense.

We are not concerned here with the politics involved, but with the curious fact that whereas at the outset Seretse and Ruth would have been hard put to it to live a comfortable social life in England, except in their own very select and chosen circle, as exiles they were received with warmth. In the heat of the political excitement and with traditional sympathy for the underdog, regardless of its pedigree, racial considerations were forgotten, as was the fact that Ruth had been a typist.

But this did not make their marriage much easier, for both wanted to return to Bechuanaland and for some years there was not even a remote possibility of this. It was a situation that might have upset any marriage, but in this case it brought out certain qualities in both Ruth and Seretse that not only saved their marriage but made it all the stronger. One such quality was that of honesty, so foreign to British public life. With regard to public opinion the Khamas moved and lived as openly as if it did not exist, and when they eventually found a nondiscriminating landlord they settled down to iron out the difficulties of private life in a neighborhood that received them with mixed feelings. Each, in an effort to make it easier for the other in these early days of marriage, went out of his way to understand the other's point of view. At one point Seretse was more English than Ruth, and she more African than he, and when a child was born, Jaqueline, she had the wisdom, if not all the advantages, of both worlds.

Another such marriage, but without any such political difficulties at the outset, was between Joseph Appiah, a relative of the Ashantihene (King of the ancient Ashanti nation in Ghana), and Peggy Cripps, daughter of Sir Stafford Cripps, the British politician. In this case both parties could claim not only wealth but family fame, and both were intellectual as well as social equals. They met in London, where Joseph was a law student, but they fully realized the implications of their attachment to each other and made very sure of their feelings before they committed themselves. When they were sure of their feelings they took stock of every other consideration. Peggy went to Ghana for some months to live with Joseph's family knowing that if she married him she would have to live in Ghana and bring up any children they might have there, rather than in England. She wanted to be sure that she could live and keep her health in what was, for her, a totally new environment, in a different climate and with different food. She also wanted to be sure that she would be able to find a place for herself in the community in which she would live. Only when she returned to England did the two become engaged.

They were married a year later in a highly fashionable London church. Most of Peggy's family, unlike Sir Stafford, were true-blue Tories, but they turned out in force and in full dress. Joseph's family and friends likewise turned out in force in their own much more colorful national costumes. Hardly a word of criticism was breathed on either side and the couple returned to Ghana. Both took a prominent part in the social and political life of their country with absolutely no disabilities on grounds of their marriage. Their only difficulty has been Joseph's political difference of opinion with

Nkrumah which ultimately ended, as they knew it probably would, with his arrest. Yet in spite of this, and in spite of the unexpected threat that Joseph might have to face a capital charge, Peggy's reply when it was suggested that she return to England was that she was now a Ghanean, that Ghana was her home, and that she was going to stay.

These are more than just stories of happy marriages. They indicate, for one thing, how shallow is the racial aspect of public opinion toward mixed marriages; for the same people who decried the influx of Negroes into England on the grounds that it would lead to intermarriage, which they thought of as immoral or as racial suicide, took a strange pride in the success of these two marriages, simply because they involved well known and popular personalities who faced enormous difficulties and overcame them. What is even more important, however, is not that the marriages were a success in that these two families became perfectly integrated into the societies where they made their homes, but that they have evolved new values for themselves, out of both necessity and desire, and have by their example alone passed these values on to others. There was no political opposition to the Appiahs' marriage, but just as with the Khamas' there was some personal opposition from both within and without the immediate families concerned. This had to be met and resolved, for purely personal reasons of family respect on the English side, but for even more compelling reasons on the African side, where family loyalties are so much more exacting and binding. There were also differences of attitude and opinion that implied differences of understanding, and to make the marriages successful the individuals had each to make certain adjustments to the situation. For instance, while Peggy Cripps had a way of saying exactly what she thought, clearly and directly, Joseph Appiah delighted in appearing to say the exact opposite of what he meant and in the most obscure and roundabout way possible. Perhaps this was a technique he had learned from his law studies, or from his study of British diplomacy. Each attitude indicated different values that were by no means superficial or easily altered, and the significant thing is that instead of trying to alter them, Peggy and Joseph merely found a third and higher value that they shared in common, in light of which their different attitudes toward directness of speech *did* become superficial. It was this higher value perhaps that made it possible, or even necessary, for Joseph to risk his life, and which gave him the strength to do so, and the very same ideal has given Peggy the determination to remain in Ghana with her children in the face of political opposition and threat.

The Khamas and the Appiahs are not the only such couples by any means. I cite them merely because I know them and know something of what was involved. Nor is the actual act of intermarriage necessarily a solution in itself, but it does point very sharply toward certain aspects of the conflict between the two ways of life that we are considering. These people, and others like them, have managed to make a thorough success of their marriages because on each side sacrifices had to be made, and equally on each side there had to be refusals to sacrifice. The adjustments of ways of life were relatively easy to make: Peggy Cripps was able to abandon the social graces demanded by London society and adopt those expected in Kumasi; Ruth Williams proved herself perfectly capable of acting with all the restraint and dignity required of her as a chief's wife. But there had to be a common meeting ground, spiritual as well as intellectual, that would make a free interchange of ideas possible not only between the individuals but between them and the communities in which they lived. To live in Africa as a European is easy enough, but to live there as a European *and* as an African by marriage requires something special. There is a different way of thinking, arising out of the different beliefs and values, that can not be adopted as though it were just another custom. There are many who have recognized this fact, administrators, settlers, scholars and scientists among them, and many have recognized it as a problem that has to be solved. Few have managed to do so, and perhaps it can be done only by those motivated by a force as powerful—and as clean—as love. The problem is the same at the national level as it is at the individual level, and so perhaps is the solution.

There are cases where the European party to a mixed marriage has consciously tried to "go native" because of the certainty of nonacceptance by the white population, and such cases are generally disastrous. There was one such instance in Stanleyville involving one of the oldest inhabitants, that of a man who had settled there when it was not much more than a small trading post. I do not know his early history, but when I met him, over ten years ago, he had already been married to his African wife for long enough to have a flourishing breed of grandchildren. He lived at the edge of the white residential quarter in what had once been a fine, large house but had by then become dilapidated, the gardens overgrown. Where there had once been formal beds of European flowers there were now native pawpaw and plantain trees, and pineapples sprouted indiscriminately here and there. The old man had been impoverished by the demands of all his newly acquired relatives—demands that were perfectly justifiable under the local African system of values but which were insupportable in an urban economy. He stuck to his principles, and to his attempt to be as African as his wife, and allowed himself slowly to be ruined, renting one room after another in a vain attempt to make ends meet. His strange ménage was not unhappy, but neither was it happy, and in no way was it integrated with either the black or the white society of Stanleyville. On the contrary it set up, as it was inevitably destined to do, a third isolated group—that of the mulatto. Nothing was solved by the marriage. The two worlds, black and white, remained as far apart as ever and the third, the mulatto world, was as removed from either parent world as they were from each other, and all because there was no basis for a free interchange of ideas and beliefs, only a futile attempt at identification.

So also in the wider realm of culture contact the adoption of new customs or the adaptation of old is by itself insufficient, because it is fundamentally superficial. There has to be something much deeper, and that something is a completely new sense of values that is neither adopted nor adapted, but spontaneously developed in the new mixed environment. Appeals are frequently heard for "tolerance," but this is not what is wanted at all, for tolerance implies the rigid adherence to one's own point of view, implying its superiority, while merely allowing others to hold a different, and therefore inferior, point of view. What comes from a real marriage between the two worlds is more than that, even more than mutual understanding and acceptance. The result of such a union is understanding put into practice, a spontaneous activity that is full of the freshness and honesty and beauty of youth, heir to the experience and wisdom of the two parent worlds.

There is little doubt that the kind of synthesis that comes from the intermarriage between two individuals is also appearing, though slowly, in some African societies. But it is appearing unequally in the various aspects of social life, so that there is still no totally new social framework into which the "integrated" African can fit. The trend, however, is there. The mere desegregation of formerly exclusive clubs, schools, political institutions and churches is an indication of direction rather than an achievement, but nonetheless it makes the achievement possible. This is particularly true in the fields of elementary education and sport, because in each case the participants share common values. Young children who have not learned otherwise, accept or reject each other for reasons less whimsical than color preference. They grow up accustomed to judging people by the standards they share in common at school. When they eventually learn about "race," it is almost accidentally, and it is certainly incidental, and the common values remain unless the children are removed from contact and have their upbringing continued in more rigidly racist communities. In the normal course of events, in a modern African city where education is desegregated, when a child reaches adulthood the bonds are already firmly enough established to prevent the overgrowth of the racist belief that he is naturally and inherently superior to others. This little is in itself no small step forward. Similarly, in the world of sport, individuals tend to lose their race consciousness, but they also develop a more positive spirit of camaraderie through co-operative endeavor —unless of course even sport is segregated, as it is in South Africa.

In everyday social life social conventions segregate one class of peoples from another, and although even in unsegregated communities this still runs largely on racial lines, it is because of the present and temporary economic and intellectual supremacy of the whites rather than because of any belief in inherent disabilities. In such a community the proportion of European to African members of a club may seem disproportionately high, but that is only looking at it with racist eyes. The significant proportions are those between rich and poor, educated and uneducated, professional men and laborers, and these proportions cut across racial boundaries in the new African cities, and color is barely even thought of, still less mentioned, as a social qualification.

In this way people of both races are for the first time learning to live side by side, sharing the same way of life. For the first time they are able to discuss their differences of opinion, and each feels strong enough to hold his own if he wishes to. Here is a fertile ground for an interchange of ideas that can give rise to a new social synthesis.

In the economic field the marriage between the two worlds comes less easily, particularly in rural areas. With mechanization and industrialization come necessary and inevitable social changes, sometimes called reforms. This process is too rapid and fixed in nature to tolerate any compromise. It not only upsets the whole traditional labor pattern and the associated relationship between the sexes as economic entities, but it also throws overboard the very concept of the family as an economic unit. Insofar as the notion of family is not one that can easily be abandoned, even one aspect of it, to that extent the modern economic system is accepted only as a necessary evil. A cash economy, which is the only kind we really know, seems to us to be the only kind there can or should be. Yet the introduction of a cash economy alone into a rural community in Africa can destroy the very foundations of morality by undermining interfamily and intrafamily systems of obligations and privileges.

The same thing happens with political systems. We feel that our form of democracy is the only reasonable form of government, and we introduce it because it is the only form that makes sense to us and that we know how to handle. We are aware that it creates certain difficulties for the African, but these are generally put down to a lack of understanding on his part, or to his lack of intelligence and ability. But again, the traditional political systems of Africa were most frequently founded on the concept of the family, and their destruction adds to the destruction of the whole indigenous system of values. The old government is relatively easily replaced by the new, but something just as important, if not more so, is irretrievably lost in the process. It can not be regained under the new system any more than the system of values that underlie our concept of government can or should be adopted.

With independence, various African nations are facing this problem. In Ghana, where Parliament sat in British style with the opposition benches facing those of the government, this form of seating has been abolished. The model British constitution which the British bequeathed to the new nation is being progressively abandoned. Outside Ghana there are cries of "Shame!" and accusations of dictatorship. *Dictatorship* is a very inexact term today, and could perhaps be applied where people least expect it. There *is* a strong central authority in Ghana, essential to prevent the chaos that would otherwise have followed the removal of the no less strong central colonial government. The removal of the opposition benches and the imprisonment of opponents to the central government does not mean the removal of opposition. The house is no longer divided, the country is united under one nominal leader, but in fact this is a revival of the old concept of the nation as a single family. Within that family any member may state his views freely without being considered a traitor to his "party," without being censured by the party whip, without being refused official support by the party at the next elections. Nkrumah's cabinet members themselves are free to stand up and oppose any motion they see fit, as in fact they do. The one thing one must not be opposed to in present-day Ghana, as in traditional Ghana, is the person of the leader, nor must it be brought into disrepute. The traditional head of state was in a sense sacred, and could do no wrong. This is precisely the burden of the many songs of praise sung to Nkrumah. But the traditional head of state also had a responsibility to his people, and was bound by the voice of the people to a considerable extent. So again is Nkrumah.

This is not an attempt to justify what is going on in Ghana, it is only an attempt to understand it, and to see its possibilities, and its dangers.

At whatever level we look, at whatever aspect of social life, the superficiality of acculturation is evident, and nothing can be done about it. The remaining question, and perhaps the most vital one, is whether or not to be satisfied with a proven, if cumbersome, governmental system and whether or not to attempt to give it some deeper foundations by adopting the corresponding values. The alternative to imposing a wholesale adoption of the western pattern of life is the evolution of a new way of thought, a way that takes both worlds into consideration. This is no easy task, and there are few who are either interested or qualified to consider it. It would also consume a critical amount of that most precious commodity— time. On one side there is an immobility of tradition coupled with a low educational level and lack of critical ability (due entirely to the paucity of schools), and on the other side is the narrow dog- matism of Christianity against which reason is, in any case, power- less. There can be no argument, for instance, where the Christian church teaches, as does the Dutch Reformed Church in South Africa, that black Africans are the accursed children of Ham, condemned to be hewers of wood and drawers of water, servants of servants. In such a situation change can come only from a change of belief, and how to achieve this other than by patient example is difficult to see.

The kind of confusion of thought that arises from this situation is easily seen in a conversation I had with a small group of West Africans, mostly connected with the United Nations, in New York. All were nominally Christian except for an architect who was an agnostic. One praised the government of Ghana for the abolition of a divided political house, thus emphasizing the notion of the single family and family solidarity. The architect countered with the remark that this was not much good if the same undivided government sponsored elaborate housing projects that made family life, in the West African sense of the extended family, physically impossible. He himself had been working on designs for housing projects that would deal with the same problem of urban over- population, but still taking the family concept into account and making a corporate existence possible. But the contracts had been given to European-type projects of "proven success"—the success of course having been proven in Europe, not in Africa. An econo- mist at the same gathering said that the notion of family was destined to disappear anyway because modern economic systems made co-operation along family lines unworkable and even undesirable. The only African woman present promptly (along with the architect) questioned the validity of this attitude, asking which was more important, a "modern" economic system or the family; and here opinion broke up and divided into irreconcilable factions.

In fact, this is the point where opinion inevitably divides, for the old concept of the family *is* untenable in modern Africa. Yet it is the source of all morality and spiritual pride and strength, even to many of the African Christians. Even the most sophisticated Africans are coming to realize that perhaps the advantages offered by the modern western form of civilization are at times outweighed by disadvantages. But even as the opportunities for intermarriage between two individuals are limited, so are opportunities for intermarriage between the two ways of life. In the cold realm of practice the one militates too strongly against the other. The African family can not survive under a western economic and political system, and if the family can not survive neither can the values. It is a question of deciding which is the more valuable, a way of life or a way of thought. Intermarriage can be an act of faith in a way of thought, an expression of belief and of trust; and if it is these things then it is strong enough to be able to disregard the accepted way of life. When it has this inner strength it succeeds, and makes for itself its own place in society and wins social acceptance. It is, in fact, a stimulant, if only insofar as it is a step away from social stagnation. Everything that can be said of it at a personal level can be said of it at a social level, for if the two worlds are to meet without the one destroying all that is good in the other, it can be only through the kind of understanding that comes when two individuals meet and unite as one, each changing his whole being not so much by becoming different as by becoming more nearly complete.

10

Safini

When Kasuku's younger wife gave birth to a girl the old man wept with joy. This wife was his favorite for she brought laughter and happiness into his old age at a time when he thought the world was full only of sorrow. It was so full of sorrow that he had taken just two wives when he decided that it was no good taking any more. His father had enjoyed some ten or eleven and Kasuku remembered with pleasure the fun it had been having so many mothers, and being able to run to them all and know that he would be fondled and fussed over. He had made up his mind that he would bring up a family to be equally happy, that he would take twenty or thirty wives, and that all his children would be proud of their father and everyone would point to him as a man of wealth and a model of contentment—a man to be envied—a man whose seed would grow and multiply and pass his name on for uncountable generations, a man who was favored by the ancestors.

But the white men who ruled the country from their brick houses at Mafia had said that it displeased them that one man should have so many wives, and they withdrew favors so that those who were wealthy with wives appeared poor in terms of favor, and lost the respect of their less fortunate brothers. And the white men of God taught all the children that to have more than one wife was evil, so that children came to have contempt for their fathers. And so those who had been blessed by the ancestors, and had brought them the blessings of many children in return, they became the unfortunate ones.

Kasuku had seen this happen, and after he had taken his second wife he was told that if he took another he would be put in prison on some pretext or other—and there were always plenty of pretexts because there were so many new laws that nobody could be expected to remember them all, and they made no sense, so one could not even reason them out. Just why, for instance should one not eat okapi flesh and wear its beautiful skin? The Pygmies were always killing them in the forest and bringing him the meat. Should he just let it rot? And the skins were better than any antelope skin. Yet he would be put in prison if he was seen with one over his shoulders. And why, on the other hand, did everyone have to plant that dreadful plant that grew up and gave the womenfolk so much trouble when it was time to pick the white fluffy balls the white man called cotton? Who could eat that? And everyone knew that it was bad for the ground, which became exhausted quickly enough anyway. When he had asked, once, that simple question, "Why?" he had been threatened with a stick and told, "Because I am the administrator, that's why!"

Kasuku had learned that it was better not to question and not to argue, so he had taken no more wives, and had grown old with only two. But as he grew old he began to care less and less about what the white man said. It still made no sense to him. And now he had children to look after the plantations and to provide him with food and clothing, so he consulted his two wives, who both agreed that it would be wonderful to have another co-wife, for they too were getting old, and they knew Kasuku had his eye on young Asofi. And even when Kasuku married Asofi and showed her so much favoritism they did not mind, because she did so much work, and took such good care of the old man, who really was getting very demanding. Only when Asofi became pregnant did they feel just a little jealous, and they put out the story that it had not been Kasuku, but one of Asofi's former lovers.

Kasuku was too delighted to care, however, and when the girl child was born he named her Safini, after his own sister. This was something of an innovation, as normally the girl child would have been named from her mother's family, and everyone shook their heads and said that if Kasuku did not uphold the traditions who would?

Safini grew up with her young mother and her old father in very happy circumstances and she grew to be beautiful.

It was just after she had been cursed with the first appearance of moon-blood that she set eyes on the man everyone called Bwana Banduki because he always carried so many guns. She had heard many strange tales about him, and she was surprised that he was not as white as the administrator, for everyone had said he was white. Perhaps it was because he was covered all over with so much hair. She really never got over her curiosity that his body should have been so completely covered, just like that of a chimpanzee. The other boys and men she knew only had hair on the top of their heads and between their legs.

But the strangest thing about Bwana Banduki was that he had been brought up among her own people, the Bafwamiti, and had even been through the initiation school with other boys of the same age. He spoke the language just like one of themselves. Only he had no home, and he owned no plantation. He traveled about a great deal, always taking one or two other white men with him. For weeks at a time they would remain in the forest, finally coming out with skins and antelope heads, and sometimes with elephant tusks. Occasionally the administrator went with him, and he was plainly considered an important person among his own people.

Bwana Banduki was, in fact, a white hunter. His real name was Jean-Paul, and his father had been one of the early survey team employed by the Congo government. Both his parents had thought it a good thing for their son to grow up with the people among whom they lived and worked, and were only mildly surprised when he said that his friends wanted him to join them in the initiation school. But for Jean-Paul it was more than a mere gesture; he knew that this was where he belonged, and he wanted to belong completely. When he was in his late teens he took to hunting as a career, feeling that this was the one way he could be sure of always making his living in the forest.

He had long thought of making Kasuku's village his headquarters, and he was pleased to find the old man agreeable. He was also pleased to find that young Safini was no longer the baby he remembered, but an exceptionally pretty and rapidly maturing young girl.

It was only three years after establishing himself in a neat little mud house, not far from Kasuku's, that he decided to ask the old man's permission to marry Safini. He knew that no white girl would want to live the way he did, and in any case he now felt almost more at home among the Bafwamiti than he did with his own people.

It seemed that Kasuku had been holding onto life for just this moment. He had been growing weaker for some years, and for a long time he had been unable to walk more than five paces without sitting down to rest. He was nearly blind, but he was more happy than ever because Asofi had given him new life . . . and a daughter. He told Jean-Paul that he could not wish for a finer son, and only asked that he look after Safini and give her lots of good clothes and beat her if she misbehaved. He asked Jean-Paul if he would take other wives, and when he was told no, that Safini would be his only wife, the old man sank back in his cushions with a slight sigh of disappointment. He called his daughter and told her that he wanted her to marry Bwana Banduki, to which Safini replied that she would do whatever her father said. This very meekness was as good as saying that she was delighted, and the old man gave his blessing. He died just before the wedding, but not before he had arranged for Jean-Paul to pay a handsome dowry of goats and cloth, a dowry that would do the girl justice and make everyone see how highly she was esteemed and respected.

For several years Safini and Jean-Paul lived in great happiness amongst the Bafwamiti. Every now and then he would go off to Stanleyville or to Bunia to meet wealthy white tourists, who paid him to take them through the forest and show them how to shoot the wild game, particularly the elephant and the *bongo*.* After a few weeks he was home again with his Safini, and together they worked to make their home even prettier than it was, planting all manner of flowers in the little border that ran right around, front and back. They also worked together in the plantation, where they grew all sorts of strange fruits and vegetables that Safini had never even seen before.

Sometimes Safini wondered why her husband never brought any of these white men home, but he explained that they were not really his friends, that they merely paid him and he was more of a servant; and in this way she understood it would have been improper to offer them hospitality. But she could not understand what kind of white men they were, because nobody else treated Jean-Paul as a servant—even the administrator, who was a frequent visitor to their home, seemed to look up to him. Safini began to resent these people who treated her husband as an inferior, because one day she saw three of them standing beside the government rest house. They were not smartly dressed, like Jean-Paul, and even worse, they were dirty. Even from the road her nostrils twitched at the smell of sweat. They were arguing among themselves as to how much they should pay a young boy who had

* *A forest antelope, not so much a rare animal as one that is seldom seen.*

brought them some eggs, and this was what really struck Safini, for she had been taught that important people never argue among themselves in front of inferiors, let alone quibble with them over money. She felt she knew now the real reason why her husband never brought such men home. He was ashamed that his own people could be like this.

The rest of the villagers had no such problems, and so it was difficult for Safini to talk to her friends about these matters. When she did they just laughed at her and said that anyone who had so much happiness as she did was bound to have some problems as well. And Safini was happy, very much so. Unlike other girls, she had not had to leave her home village when she married, so she was still among her own people; and she had a wonderful husband. She was proud to see him at the market, sitting down under the old Mbau tree to drink palm wine with the men as she went about her business. He was so very well liked by everyone, it seemed.

Safini's only unhappiness was that her husband did not want her to have any children. She tried every way she could to persuade him otherwise, but it was no good. When she asked him why, he merely told her that she would not understand, but that he just knew it to be right. And being what she was, Safini trusted her husband, and tried to make up for it by loving him all the more.

Then there came a time when the administrator and a number of other government people came to visit their home almost every week. Safini enjoyed cooking for them, and the administrator nearly always brought her some little present which he would slip into her hand as she shyly approached the table to serve the meal to the men. And afterwards, when the meal was over and the men were talking together in a language Safini did not understand, she used to sit in the shadows and watch, in case they had any needs. Then too the administrator or one of the others sometimes came and chatted with her, joking and teasing, and paying her compliments on her cooking. That made Safini very proud, because although she knew she was a good cook, it gave her great pleasure to be able to tell her friends all the nice things such great and important men as the administrator had said about her food.

Safini knew from the frequency of the visits that something was happening that her husband was not telling her, and she began to be afraid. She several times heard mention of places she knew to be many miles away, right by the Panga River. No Bafwamiti liked to even mention that country, because the people who lived there had been their hereditary enemies right up to the time the Belgians came and prevented them from fighting with weapons. The Belgians had not stopped the feeling of hostility, however, and the battle was still being waged, as strongly as ever. The BaSinga were much more powerful witches than the Bafwamiti, and they had many more sorcerers and a much greater knowledge of medicine that brought not only pain, but death. Even to mention the BaSinga, or their country, was to invite disaster, and Safini felt her home being slowly filled with evil.

One day Jean-Paul came back home from a week in Stanleyville. He told Safini that the government wanted him to take charge of a botanical research station that was being set up on the banks of the Panga River. The station would number about a hundred workers to start with, and there would be accommodation for half a dozen or more scientists. The research work would be directed by the resident scientist, a Belgian named Henri Dupont, who was already in Stanleyville with his wife; but Jean-Paul was to be in charge of the station as such, with full administrative powers. He was to leave as soon as possible to clear the ground and put up the necessary buildings . . . he wanted Safini to come with him.

Safini, like most of her people, had never traveled beyond the borders of the tribal territory, and it took Jean-Paul a long time to convince her that the countryside by the Panga River was just the same as it was right there. But Safini was not so worried about the countryside as she was about the people. Her husband assured her that the BaSinga were not nearly as bad as the Bafwamiti believed them to be, and he personally knew the chief and many of the people in Ndola, which would be the nearest village to the station. They were all his friends, and they would be her friends. Comforted to some extent by this, and by the assurance that she would be able to return to Mbau whenever she wanted for a visit, Safini subdued her fears. But when she was getting everything ready for the journey and she came across the small leather locket that had been tied around her neck as a child, to protect her from evil spirits, she carefully restrung it and fastened it in place. She was a little ashamed, because living with Jean-Paul she had grown away from such superstitions. But when he saw it, he did not make fun of her. He just smiled and put his arm around her and told her she was going to love her new home. He would build her a new house, whatever size she wanted, and she could have as many servants as she needed. He would not have to go away on hunting trips, they could be together all the time.

The clearing work went quickly enough, as the villagers of Ndola and from all around quickly learned that the new Bwana Mukubwa, The Great Master, paid well and did not use a whip. This was something new to those used only to working on the road gangs. Scaffolding was erected around the huge mahogany trees, and they came crashing down, one after another. The small sawmill brought in from Stanleyville cut the lumber into planks, and the rest was either stored as firewood, or just burned. Jean-Paul did not have all the trees cut down. He left them standing here and there, to cast their shade around the neat log cabins he built below. He had only three trained carpenters, two from the BaSinga tribe, and one, Lukamba, from a remote tribe on the far side of Bafwamiti country, the notorious BaKeti.* But Lukamba

---

* *The BaKeti have a widespread and evil reputation for sorcery.*

had been brought up in a mission school, where he had learned carpentry, and in many ways he seemed more European than he did African. It was largely with his help that Jean-Paul soon had half a dozen men capable of measuring and cutting wood for the others to assemble in the building of the house and the making of the necessary furniture.

At first Safini and her husband lived in a small hut built for them by the station workers in the manner of an ordinary village hut, with baked mud walls and a leaf roof. But theirs had a large veranda and a separate kitchen. It was close to Lukamba's hut, and Safini grew to know Lukamba and his wife well, and to like them. She had little to do with the other workers, because she had insisted on bringing three of her own villagers with her as servants, and they also acted as friends. In this way she had no need even to talk to the BaSingas. But Jean-Paul soon had their proper house built, not far from the banks of the Panga. He had it surrounded by a fence, which Safini thought was unfriendly, and when he explained that it was necessary to discourage the station workers and their wives from hanging around the kitchen she thought that odd too, but she did not mind as she did not particularly like any of the workers except Lukamba.

The house was made of rough-hewn logs, and it had large windows facing the river. There were four good-sized rooms in it; a large sitting room, an office, their bedroom and a guest room. The furniture was all made in traditional village style, but enlarged and adapted to their needs, with chairs made in the way that Lukamba had been taught at the Mission School. Safini was a little bewildered by the size and elegance of the new home, but it made her very proud. As soon as it was finished Jean-Paul set to work to build a house nearby for Henri Dupont. He made it in the same style, but took much more care with the finishing of the interior, to make it as much like a European home as possible. He designed the furniture himself, and had glass fitted to the windows.

His own windows he left open, with wooden shutters that could be closed during a storm. The low overhanging eaves formed a wide veranda all around the house, protecting the rooms both from the heat of direct sunlight and from the rain that fell almost every afternoon throughout the year. When all was ready, and the workers' village was completed not far away, Jean-Paul sent word to Stanleyville for Monsieur Dupont to come and see that everything was to his liking.

Safini had found plenty to do at first, clearing a garden with the help of her friends from Bafwamiti so that in a few months they would have their own supply of bananas and manioc, peanuts and beans. She also helped with the furnishings, making drapes for the windows from trade cloths she bought at the little store at Ndola, and stuffing cushions and mattresses with locally grown cotton. But then she found time began to weigh heavily. It seemed to press down on her, making it more and more difficult to pass each hour, until the days seemed painfully long. She would walk to Ndola with her friends and pass time at the store there, and she would watch from a distance some of the dancing that was nearly always going on near the chief's house. But she and her friends from Bafwamiti were never invited to take part, and the chairs that were brought for them to sit on were always placed apart. Safini, with her natural kindness of heart, put it down to their respect for her husband, and in turn remained more aloof than she wanted to.

She waited to see Monsieur Dupont and his wife with eagerness, and spent many hours touching up their home. On the day they were to arrive she put flowers in each of the rooms, something that her husband had taught her that all Europeans liked. When they drove up and got out of their car at the entrance to the station, Safini was one of the first to see them. She had just returned from Ndola, and she ran to tell her husband. Jean-Paul told her to get the food ready, and went out to greet the newcomers. But the food had been ready for some time, so Safini just watched from the kitchen compound as the party walked toward the house. She heard Henri Dupont talking loudly in a high-pitched voice, and was surprised that he seemed to be arguing with her husband about something. Lukamba, who understood French, was also watching. He told her that the newcomer was complaining about not being able to drive right up to the door, and was saying that a proper road would have to be put through. It seemed a small matter to argue about. Safini set the food on the table.

The three sat down on the veranda for drinks, served by Jean-Paul, while Safini made sure everything was in order inside. Then they came in, strangely silent, and took their places at the table. As usual Safini came to serve them, it being her custom not to eat with her husband unless they were alone. She hesitated, waiting to be introduced, but Jean-Paul just motioned her to serve the meal. It was eaten in silence, and Safini noticed with pleasure that although they looked at the food with distaste, Monsieur Dupont and his wife ate heartily enough once they tasted it.

After dinner they went back to the veranda for coffee, and again Safini waited to be introduced, and again Jean-Paul motioned her away.

But Safini was not one to worry about such things. She had heard them arguing, and thought that must be the reason her husband was so forgetful. So she introduced herself. Shyly she came up with her own cup of coffee, and as there was no other chair on the veranda, she squatted down near Madame Dupont and asked her, in KiNgwana, if she liked the house her husband had built for her. Madame Dupont looked at her in embarrassment and said it was very quaint. She then looked at Henri Dupont and she said she would like to go and see their own house. She stood up, turned her back on Safini and walked down the veranda steps. Jean-Paul seemed about to say something, then he changed his mind and turned to Monsieur Dupont and said he would show them around at once. He took Safini's hand and, still talking to Monsieur Dupont, told him how his wife had helped to furnish the house. He spoke in KiNgwana, but Monsieur Dupont replied in French, and Safini could not understand.

It was only when they got to the new house that Safini began to comprehend. Madame Dupont walked from room to room, touching things gingerly, and then she spoke, loudly and clearly to her husband, in KiNgwana. "But it is just like a native hut—we can't live here—we are not animals!" Safini was about to turn and run, but Jean-Paul held onto her tightly. "Madame," he said, "it is a great deal more comfortable than the house I built for my wife and myself; we could do no more in the time——" Madame Dupont interrupted, "That may be, but *I* am not a savage." She turned to her husband, and spoke again in French. They left shortly afterwards.

When her husband explained to her, later that day, that many Europeans felt as the Duponts did about white men having African wives, Safini found it difficult to understand. She could understand their not wanting to have to walk a hundred yards from the car to the house, she could understand their preferring a brick house to a wooden one, and she knew enough of Europeans to realize that they can get extraordinarily ill-tempered over such little things. But how could they be annoyed by Jean-Paul's having an African wife—didn't many of the men, even the administrators, have African wives? Jean-Paul explained that many of them had mistresses, but that was different, everyone could afford to ignore an association of that kind. But he and Safini were married, living openly as man and wife, and married according to tribal custom, not even according to the laws of the church.

All that Safini understood from this was that white men liked to do some things under cover of darkness of night, and pretend otherwise in the daytime. She saw quite clearly that she would have to keep herself in the background, even in her own house, when her husband's friends were visiting. This did not hurt her—they were, after all, no friends of hers—it just puzzled her. So Safini became a shadow in her own home, fading away at the sight of any European. Only in late evenings could she be a wife to her husband, and so precious was this time that she would lie awake most of the night looking at Jean-Paul as he slept. Even then there were often interruptions, as government agents came to regard the station as a convenient stopping place, and would turn up at any time of night and expect hospitality.

The Duponts came and settled down, but not in the house Jean-Paul had built for them. They imported bricks and had a fine brick house built. They cut down all the trees around it, so that it stood out in the open, catching the full glare and heat of the sun. The windows were small, like those of European houses, and the house was hot and stuffy at all times of the day and night. Jean-Paul gave the house he had built for them to Lukamba, a gesture which did not please the Duponts, but delighted Safini.

Several other Europeans came, but none of them stayed for long, and although some of them made a point of asking for Safini whenever they visited Jean-Paul's house, Safini was usually not to be found. Whenever she saw them coming she would run over to the kitchen and busy herself there. More and more she came to rely on her three friends and servants as the only people she could really talk to, apart from Lukamba and his wife. So it was a great shock to her when one day she found them all packing their bundles and preparing to leave on the weekly mail truck, back to Mbau. They were young, they said, and they wanted to dance and sleep with men, but these savages around them, the BaSinga, wanted nothing to do with them, and they wanted nothing to do with the BaSinga. It was all right for Safini, they said, she was happily married and had a husband and a fine house to live in. Safini was both too proud and too kind to argue. She prepared some food for them for the journey, and gave them presents, and told them to tell her mother that she would be back home to see her before long. But even as she spoke the words she regretted them—and for the first time fear came into her life. It was a momentary feeling, and it passed quickly. Safini stayed with her friends until the truck came, and then she stood and waved them goodbye. Long after the truck was out of sight, and only a cloud of dust remained, slowly swirling and settling down on the rough and twisting track, Safini stood there, looking with empty eyes in the direction of Mbau.

Jean-Paul told her to hire other servants, but Safini said no, she would like to do the work herself, as a wife should, and that Lukamba's wife would help her whenever needed. She would not admit that she did not want the BaSinga around her, in her home, handling her food. Knowing that they would be well paid, several of the wives of the workers came and asked Safini to hire them, and when she refused they went away and told their husbands that Safini was evil. She must be evil because she had refused to even let them into the kitchen, and it was well known that witches were afraid of others' even looking at the food they were preparing, because they were so evil themselves they thought that everyone else possessed the Evil Eye.

The extra work kept Safini busy, and Lukamba's wife was good to her, helping her whenever she needed help, and being a friend to her at all times. She and Lukamba, after all, were strangers among the BaSinga, just as was Safini herself. They went to the store at Ndola together, never alone, but they seldom went to the village market. The storekeeper wanted to make money, so he always served them—they had more money than any of the other villagers. But at the market, where women exchanged their goods rather than sell them, nobody seemed to want the fruits and vegetables that Safini brought, and when she tried to buy anything the BaSinga women just shook their heads as if they did not understand, and some of them drew cloths over their food lest it be cursed by a glance from the foreign witch.

Safini told her husband nothing of this. She only asked him once, timidly, if they could not go back to Mbau and live there as they had done once, so happily. Jean-Paul laughed at her, and said that he was making more money now than he had ever made before, and life was better for them than it could ever be at Mbau. So much so, he said, that he felt it time that they had children. The words that once would have filled Safini with joy now only made her more frightened than ever. And when her stomach began to swell, Safini fell ill.

She was up at the store at Ndola, buying some cloth; as usual there were a number of men sitting around outside, drinking palm wine. They looked pointedly at her belly as she passed by, and whispered among themselves. When she came out one of them said to the others, loud enough for her to hear: "The Bafwamiti circumcise foreigners and allow them to marry their daughters, but no child so conceived on our land will live—our laws forbid it. It is an offense to the ancestors and brings danger to us all."

It soon became the talk of the whole village, and of the station, that the witch doctor had cursed Safini's child to die, and that she would be barren the rest of her life for having desecrated BaSinga soil with her uncleanliness. People began not only to avoid her, but rather to pretend not to see her. As she passed by they would look right at her and through her, as though she were not there at all. And all the time she heard whispered remarks about the fact that her child was sure to die. And what scared her more than anything was that she too knew that it would die, because she wanted it to. Jean-Paul had said finally that he could never go back to Mbau, that his whole future was here now. One day the station would grow into a flourishing little town, right in the middle of the forest, where they could have the best of both worlds, he had said. But Safini only wanted one world, and that was the world she knew and could trust, the world of the Bafwamiti. If Ndola was no place for her, it was certainly no place for her child. So it had to die.

Jean-Paul saw so little of his wife these days that he was barely aware of her fears. She had told him once, and he had laughed and said she had left all that superstition behind. She had nodded, seeing another truth in what he had said. She had not spoken of it again. Jean-Paul was overjoyed at the thought of having a child, for he too had been the object of some talk among the Europeans at the station. There were some who still looked on his marriage as being nothing more than an eccentricity, and they pointed to the lack of children as evidence. He would not dare bring up children by an African wife in such a community. But Jean-Paul did dare, and it was almost as much to prove his loyalty to his wife as it was for the sake of having a child.

The Duponts had ordered the last of the trees near their house to be cut down. It was a huge old mahogany tree that stood near the entrance of their driveway, close to the main gate. They said it could block their road if it were to fall during a storm. Jean-Paul tried to dissuade them, assuring them there was no danger, but even he finally gave in just for the sake of maintaining peace.

The men were busy cutting the upper branches one day as Safini and Lukamba's wife set out for Ndola. As they were passing by the gate, Safini suddenly stopped, and her companion asked her what was wrong. Safini said someone had called her, and it sounded like her mother . . . calling her name . . . Safini, Safini, Safini. . . . Crying out her mother's name, Safini ran toward the tree just as the branch fell.

Jean-Paul could get nobody to look after Safini except Lukamba and his wife. The three of them took turns sitting by Safini's bedside as she fought for life. There was no good calling a doctor—

she had not even been touched by the falling branch, but as it had fallen so had she, and she had lain on the ground, writhing as though the weight of the whole tree were on top of her. The workers had stood around in a cold and silent circle while Lukamba's wife ran for help. When she had been carried away, they went back to their work, and nobody even mentioned the incident again. Safini lost the baby that should have been born in a few weeks' time, and with it she lost all will to live.

In his bitterness Jean-Paul blamed the Duponts, and said it was all their fault, that they had never made the slightest move to be even courteous to his wife, and had made her sick and depressed, and finally they had insisted on having the tree cut down. The Duponts pointed out that there was not much logical connection between the two events, and that for one thing, Safini always disappeared any time they came near the house, and for another, Safini had merely fallen, the branch had not even touched her. But Jean-Paul's bitterness could not be diverted. He looked back over his time at the station, and saw in it nothing but a series of insults and slights to himself and his Safini, not only from the Duponts but from almost every other European who came by. The Duponts had even built a guest house so that passers-by would not be forced to accept hospitality in Jean-Paul's home. The spare room had remained empty then, except for one occasion on which his old friend the administrator had stayed overnight. And he remembered with increasing bitterness how his Safini had always kept fresh flowers in the spare room in case, some day, some other friend of her husband's might accept their hospitality.

Jean-Paul became more of a recluse. He ran the station as efficiently as ever, but he barely spoke a word to the Duponts or any of the other Europeans, and even the kindest of them found it best not to intrude. Safini slowly recovered, but her life had gone from her with her baby, and as soon as she was well enough she told Jean-Paul that she was going back to Mbau. She remembered how she had told her friends, when they left, that she would come back home to her mother one day. She had not meant to use the word *home,* because she had been taught that a woman's home is with her husband. But once she had spoken it she knew that it would not be so with her.

Jean-Paul had agreed readily, still not realizing what was the real nature of Safini's sickness. Shortly afterwards he resigned and accepted an offer of a post at Paulis, an important town many miles away from the station, in a completely different administrative district. He knew that several white men lived there with African wives, and formed a contented, if small, community of their own. He felt sure that Safini would be happy there.

He went to visit Safini at Mbau, and as she came out of their old house to greet him, a spark of life came to her sad eyes. It was a spark that held a question, but Jean-Paul did not understand it, and the light died as stillborn as their child. Safini simply said that she could no longer be his wife, she could no longer bear him children. The family offered him back the wealth that he had paid in expectancy of a wife that would raise his seed. Jean-Paul still did not understand, and said that he wanted Safini whether or not she could bear him children, he wanted her as a wife, as a companion, to live with him. "Where shall we live?" asked Safini, though the spark had long died. Jean-Paul began telling her all about Paulis, and how the Europeans were different there. Safini listened, and then told him to go to Paulis and settle there, if that was really what he was determined to do, and that he could write to her when he was ready. There was something in her voice that made Jean-Paul look, perhaps for the first time, beyond her words and into her heart.

She asked him if he would stay at Mbau for that night, and for that night Safini and Jean-Paul loved again as they had done years before, in the house where they had learned to love, far away from people, white and black, who did not understand the power of love, only the power of destruction. It was then that Safini told him that for the first few years she had taken medicine given to her by her mother to prevent her from conceiving. She had done it because she was afraid for the children, afraid for how her own people would accept them. "You were still called Bwana Banduki by my people," she said. "You did not carry the name of any of our families. What name would our children have carried? To what family would they have belonged? To whose ancestors would their spirits have gone?"

Jean-Paul left the next morning.

Every week the mail truck brought a letter from him to Safini, telling her of his lovely home at Paulis, and asking her if she would not come to join him. And every week the mail truck brought a letter from Safini to the man she loved, saying that she was still his wife, and would be waiting for him when he grew tired of Paulis, and came back to live among their own people, at Mbau, where they *both* belonged.

11

The Lonely African

In all the various situations in which the African has to choose between the old and the new he is in a dilemma, because he can accept neither with his whole heart and being. Where he is forced into the new, with no choice, he is still in a dilemma because of the difficulty of reconciling one way of life with a different way of thought. In the cities, with better educational facilities and more opportunities for the two worlds to meet and mingle, there can at least be a common intellectual level at which there is some chance of mutual comprehension; but despite the sophistication of the townsfolk the tribal past with its tribal attitudes is frequently still too close to be forgotten or ignored, and the new is still too new to be much more than a flimsy veneer.

Even the Africans who become Christians, ministers and priests are in a dilemma. The alternative to becoming totally divorced from their own people, cutting all material and spiritual ties, is to fall into doubt and suspicion of their chosen faith. But even though their difficulties are often the greatest, at least they retain some sense of values and standards, however confused. Together with the would-be traditionalists they alone have any firm basis of inner morality in their lives. The others are merely governed by the new forces of law and order, not by any belief in right and wrong. Expediency is the new god in African cities, and this is the new creed they have learned from the western world and the Christian church.

For a man's life to be thoroughly satisfactory there has to be some underlying conviction about life itself, be it theism or atheism, or even an intelligent, alert agnosticism. In an African city it is difficult to have any faith because of two things: a new educational system that has taught the African to regard his old faith as unscientific, superstitious nonsense, and the demonstrable hypocrisy of the followers of the God of Love who claim heaven for themselves, condemning everyone else to everlasting hellfire. It is also difficult to have faith in any particular way of life. Europeans in Africa may at one time have been envied for their apparently superior existence, for all the luxuries with which they could afford to surround themselves, for the mysterious source of power that rendered them impervious to any attack and that gave them authority over vast stretches of land. But if they were envied they were not admired, and today there is not much for which they can even be envied. The African can not be expected to have any great faith in a way of life that has done its best to exclude him, obstructing him with or without intent at almost every turn.

He may acknowledge the practical benefits that will accrue as a result of his westernization, both as an individual and as a member of a new nation, but even his materialism is halfhearted, for the western way also brings many inevitable disadvantages with which the African is unable to deal. These disadvantages concern old ways, those most deeply rooted in tradition, highly valued, but which can not possibly continue under the new economic, social and political pressures. In nearly all areas the family is one such way of life, for the African family *is* a way of life, and in the manner in which it is understood by Africans it is totally impracticable in the new westernized cities. In some regions polygamy is another institution of deep significance outlawed in urban communities, though its roots may underlie the whole system of traditional law and order and morality. The traditional concept of justice dies hard; although the urban African readily enough gives over his body to the new system his heart does not accept it nor does he really understand it. Too often it goes against his whole notion of right and wrong, or good and evil. His adherence to modern laws, then, can at the best be only superficial. Similarly with the political system; it is too far removed from the traditional belief in authority derived from the family-at-large, that is, the ancestors. Sometimes attempts are made to bridge the gap by giving the new political leaders honorary ancestral status. Nkrumah is referred to as ' Father of the Nation," and he is further deified by singing in his praise Christian hymns, with Nkrumah appearing as a savior in the place of Christ.

In the cities the African loses his tribal sense more quickly and easily than in the country, and he has a greater opportunity for feeling himself a part of the new and wider political unit, the nation. It helps to be able to look on a leader, such as Nkrumah, as if he were a tribal chief; but again it is just a matter of practical expediency. There was an inner strength in the old system that is still lacking in the new.

There are, then, inherent conflicts in the new way that prevent complete acceptance, and this is not surprising considering how it has been imposed from without, with not the slightest consideration for the old way. At the same time it is obvious that the old has gone for good, and in the cities the Africans have come to look upon it with shame, so that it is no longer even a source of pride, let alone of moral or spiritual strength.

A number of these conflicts have appeared in the preceding chapters, and if they have appeared in a haphazard way, it is because that is exactly the way in which they *do* appear. There is no single problem; there are as many problems as there are individuals, for each individual has to try and make his own peace between the two worlds. The following example shows well enough how deep the conflict goes, and where its roots lie.

In a case of murder, a man named Kithuica killed another by

clubbing him to death with a piece of wood. The dead man was a friend of Kithuica's son. The accused was arrested and brought to trial in the criminal court. The first difficulty came when he pleaded guilty, and refused to accept the court's insistence that he must plead not guilty to a capital offense. He protested that he was a man, not a liar, but despite his protests the court entered a plea of not guilty.

The trial was brief, because all the witnesses agreed to the facts, as did the defendant himself. He had simply gone to his victim's house, lain in wait for him near the privy, and clubbed him to death when he came out to relieve himself. He was asked why he had done this and said that it was because the dead man had been a bad friend to his son and had refused to lend him money. Kithuica maintained that this was sufficient cause as the two young men were like blood brothers, and so were bound to help each other at all times. The court maintained otherwise and sentenced him to death.

This brought a protest not only from Kithuica's family but also an even stronger protest from the family of the man Kithuica had killed. But the sentence was carried out, and the criminal was hanged.

From the court's point of view the law had taken its proper course; there had not been a shadow of doubt as to the guilt of Kithuica, but they had given him every possible chance to explain any extenuating circumstances. In his explanation he had cited nothing that could be taken into account in his favor; the murder had been planned and executed with brutality, for no reason other than a squabble over a petty loan the victim had refused to make the murderer's son. There was not even any justification for clemency. The court's sympathy was with the murdered man's family, and they were duly surprised when their verdict met with such strong opposition from that quarter. And certainly the murderer must have been extremely surprised when one morning he was marched out of his cell to a scaffold to be hung by the neck until dead.

For the reason that he had done what he had done, and had given himself up so willingly, and convicted himself so successfully, was that he had wanted to settle a serious dispute that threatened to lead to a long blood feud. He mistook the European courtroom for an indigenous tribunal, the purpose of which is to establish justice, not simply to apply the law.

One of the greatest difficulties facing European jurists in Africa has been the absence of any written body of law. Some have committed the disastrous error of ossifying a flexible moral code by formalizing it, so that the native law could be more easily classified, understood and applied. More often the traditional system has simply been ignored, and the western code imposed. But western jurists seldom, if ever, seem to have understood that the African has a totally different concept of law, inseparable from justice, and think of a court's function not as being one of conviction and punishment, but as an attempt to find a solution to any problem brought before it.

In this particular case there was, in Kithuica's mind, a very specific problem. He was an old man, and very much a traditionalist. Although his son had not made a blood-brotherhood pact with the dead man, Kithuica regarded them as blood brothers, as in fact they themselves did. They called each other brother, and that was one piece of evidence that was rejected by the court as irrelevant. But from Kithuica's point of view it was the central point of his argument, for the use of the term *brother* implies very definite mutual obligation. They were obligations which could cost him, the father of one of the brothers, considerable wealth should his son's partner fall into need. In fact, he had helped the victim a number of times.

On several occasions he had counseled his son to demand some reciprocal attentions, more to establish his right than to even the score. Each time, according to Kithuica, his son had been refused. He had thought this bad, but had merely put it down to the modern generation of youths who form blood brotherhoods without taking the old oaths. But when his son had actually been in need and had been refused any help it became obvious that it was something more sinister than plain laxity. Kithuica, the traditionalist, thought of blood brotherhood as something more than a mere exchange society existing for mutual aid; he thought of it as making each person an indissoluble part of the other, giving each some power over the other through the mingling of bloods. The oaths were designed to prevent the abuse of that power. Now a man, not bound by the oaths and therefore unpredictable, had acquired power over his son and was obviously determined to use it for his own ends. These ends had not been made clear yet, but Kithuica suspected that they went far beyond a few petty financial gains and could emerge in any number of ways harmful not only to his son but to himself and his whole family.

There was only one way to prevent the disaster, and Kithuica took it. When questioned about the brutal nature of the murder he merely answered that everyone knew it was forbidden for Africans to own guns, the weapons with which white men kill each other so easily from a distance, and living in the city he had no use for a spear or bow and arrow. So he had used a club. He agreed that the murder had been calculated, because, he said, he was not a man who killed in a fit of temper, and in any case he was an old man and his only chance of success in the venture was by ambush.

Kithuica never for a moment thought of himself as being on trial, for he was clearly innocent of any fault. He had only done what was necessary to protect himself and his family from sorcery. But he felt that in order to prevent any further trouble, so that everyone should know that he had acted wisely, the case should be heard in public and all the evidence brought out. If he did not do this, a family feud could easily develop. The possibility of a feud was in fact the main concern of the victim's family when they protested so vigorously against Kithuica's conviction. They knew that their murdered son had done wrong and had placed Kithuica in an impossible and highly dangerous position. They felt that Kithuica had been rather too abrupt in his handling of the situation, a feeling shared by Kithuica himself, and that some compensation would have been in order. The compensation would have consisted in part of a feast given by Kithuica at which both families would have joined, re-establishing good relations.

But now the court had only aggravated the situation, adding to Kithuica's injuries by hanging him, thus giving the family more cause than ever for beginning a blood feud. The case was so completely misunderstood by the court that both parties in the trial lost all confidence in the new world around them, and today there are many who, because of similar experiences, on principle never take a case to court, even when they have been done the most obvious wrong. For them the nontraditional court is completely divorced from understanding and justice; it does not exist to help them solve their problems and live together in friendship, it merely exists to punish those who have unknowingly offended the great white master.

This kind of incident results in more than mere grievance and dissatisfaction. The full implications are best seen when a court renders what we would consider to be the fairest decision and dismisses a case because it can find no provable guilt. This in fact is the most catastrophic decision a court could make in many traditional African societies, because it implies that there are absolutely no bonds whatsoever between the plaintiff and the defendant, no common standards or values by which they can be judged. If there were such common standards and values, then obviously some solution could be found. When a court fails to find a solution and admits its failure by dismissing a case, this proves in African eyes that in the court's opinion, since there are no common values, those concerned are free to think and act toward each other as they see fit. The whole basis of morality and a common way of behavior can be destroyed in this way by what we would consider a fair juridical decision. Any semblance of social solidarity, other than that maintained through sheer fear of the force of law, collapses. The African is left alone, behaving as he does not through any inner conviction, or because of any bonds shared with his fellows, but merely because of what he considers to be expedient.

In rural areas the African has to face the same kind of conflicts and resolve the same dilemmas. But he does so from a very different viewpoint because he does not have the educational advantages, if they are such, that the urban African has. He does not have a common intellectual level with the white overlords, he does not even share the superficialities of the same culture. Unlike the urban African he has no concept of the nation, and thinks largely in tribal terms. Familiarity with local administrators may have enlarged his horizon somewhat, so that he admits of some common political bonds between his own tribe and some neighboring tribes, but he still has little or no concept of any wider unity. In point of fact, of course, in many cases the white man is the only link that holds together this amorphous agglomeration of tribes. When that link is withdrawn, as it was with indecent haste in the Belgian Congo, there should be no cause for surprise when there is immediate reversion to the normal, tribal status quo. Particularly as some 80 per cent of the population, in the case of the Congo, can be classified as tribal.

At the moment independence is rapidly passing into the hands of African nations comprised of large majorities of tribal peoples. The attitude of this rural population is of great significance, though at the moment it has little political or public voice. And in the absence of the common intellectual level possible in towns and cities, this attitude is formulated with the directness and honesty characteristic of African thought, and with a greater directness of expression than is sometimes found in urban communities.

In such a situation it is natural that there should be a great deal of misunderstanding. But whereas in urban areas it is generally and most significantly a lack of understanding of the African on the part of the European, in the rural areas it is the other way around, and the misunderstanding frequently turns to suspicion. This suspicion is directed at both the speech and the actions of the Europeans, each being frequently incomprehensible to the African in the light of his own experience in life. The way in which he attempts to understand (and he at least makes the effort, whereas the European seldom does) can only be colored by life as he knows it. In the absence of a knowledge of the European language he also has to think within the limitations of his own language, and this adds still further to the confusion.

I was once being closely questioned as to how I had made enough money to afford the long and unbelievably costly trip from the North American continent to the heart of Africa. The fact that I had been able to amass such an immense fortune so quickly was in itself suspicious. I had done the trip cheaply, and it had cost rather less than $1,000; but the people with whom I was talking considered one dollar a good week's wages, working for the white man, and this represented some nineteen years of nonstop labor. I tried to explain that I had worked in a mine in the north of Canada, and had made that much in a couple of months. They then wanted to know what kind of work called for that kind of pay, and without realizing how deep into the morass I was sinking I described the work underground. Roughly translated back from KiNgwana, the language we were speaking, my account went like this: "Every morning before the sun rose, a hundred or more of us, all living under the same roof, got up and put on many, many clothes. We even covered our mouths and noses, because it was so cold that water became solid, as hard as rock. Then we went out into the water that had fallen from the sky, not like rain, but like white ashes, and which lay for month after month covering the land and even some of the buildings. We walked from our house to where there were holes in the ground, closed by doors so that you would not fall down them. We got into boxes and were lowered into the ground, taking off our clothes because far below the ground it was warm. Down there it was dark, but we all had torches on our hats. There were paths that led for many miles, and sometimes we walked and sometimes we rode on things like the administrator's motor car, only they had no top. We dug out the rock and made great rooms underground, sending all the rock up in the boxes. White men like the color of this rock, and they pay a great deal of money for it, and that is how we got rich so quickly."

At almost every turn of the narrative I was stopped by questioning looks or remarks. The net result was that I faced the choice of being considered a great liar, or as a sorcerer endowed with the most evil powers and in league with evil spirits. The logic of their reasoning was simple enough. Translated back into English, the account looks curious, even to us. Told in KiNgwana to the Africans it was equally curious. But whereas we can equate it with our own experience and knowledge of arctic conditions, of mines, and of the value of gold, these particular Africans had no such experience or knowledge. They had never seen ice or snow, never having felt temperatures below seventy degrees. They had never seen or heard of mines, nor of gold. The only experience they did have that could be applied to my account was their knowledge that caves and holes in the ground were peopled with the most deadly and evil of all spirits. Anyone who would willingly let himself be lowered down into a hole in the ground must be in league with the spirits, and to live there all day, as we evidently did, must mean that we were up to some kind of witchcraft. This possibly explained the way in which we tricked people into giving us so much money for a lot of rock out of which came a metal that was not even any good for knives or spear blades or axes.

Luckily the snow and the ice could not be explained, and this threw the whole story into disrepute, and I let it go at that, feeling it was safer to be considered a liar. In the same way any attempt by a European to explain European concepts and ways to an African in an African language is likely to misinterpretation. This may be one reason why Christianity has such a difficult time. Heaven, which seems to be one of the central themes used to bribe Africans into acceptance of the Christian code, is generally translated into African languages giving it some connotation of the sky, a place in the clouds. If this coincided with an African belief in the existence of such a place that would be fine, but usually it does not. Anywhere that man can not freely go, be it the sky or the underground regions, or even the territories beyond the tribal boundaries, is thought of as being peopled with spirits and ghosts. Such beliefs as these are that suppose a specific place where man continues to live after death, generally indicate a distant terrain similar to that inhabited by the living. Nobody in his right senses wants to go and live in the sky. The Scriptures translated literally into an African language must look at least as odd to the African as they do to us when translated back, equally literally, into English. Sometimes the meaning becomes distorted, sometimes reversed; sometimes it has connotations in African experience fully as unfortunate as my innocent story about the holes in the ground. Single words or phrases, by association with African experience, take on very different meanings.

Thus John 1:1, translated back into English, would read: "At first a Word came, and the Word came together with God, and the Word became the God." Already theologians would quibble, in this simple sentence, with the absence of the definite article in the first phrase. And they might take real exception to the final phrase, implying that the Word became that particular God instead of stating that it actually *was* God. But the African listening to the African version of the above would get an even more different impression. In light of his own experience, and of his experience of the European usage of his language, he would be most likely to understand the following:

"In the beginning there was a great argument, and the argument came with God, and the argument entered into God." And judging by the multitude of missionaries and sects and their differences of opinion, this is not an unreasonable interpretation of God.

Alternatively, the offending word *neno* could be translated "message," or "matter," both of which are more common interpretations of the same root than the intended translation, "word." Thus the African may well demand what was the argument about. Is that why there are so many arguments about God between different Men of God? Or he might wonder just what the mysterious message was that somehow became involved, rather ungrammatically, with God, who came with it.

This particular passage would not be likely to cause any serious suspicion, but it would cause misunderstanding, or at the best would have little meaning for the African. To be translated effectively the translation would have to vary for each specific language and culture. In the area from which the biographies in this book are taken, and in the language from which the above translation was made, it would have to read something like this:

"Even before the days of our ancestors a great sound filled the forest and all the regions beyond it. The sound was a voice, and God was inside the voice, just as the voice was inside God." This is all necessary because there are certain limitations to credulity, and the Bible, literally translated, takes on the appearance of either a rather stupid lie or else a comic make-believe story. As it is, it is stretching things to suggest that there was any time before the ancestors, with whom all things began, or that there is any world beyond the forest, beyond which all things end; and many Biblical stories, no matter how well translated, strain credulity to the breaking point.

There is a very real problem of communication, then, when it comes to translating European concepts into an African language, particularly those that are relatively simple and limited. But equally important are the opportunities for misunderstanding not only language, but action. In the same manner that many of the ways in which Africans behave are misunderstood by Europeans, so many of the ways in which Europeans behave are misunderstood by Africans. And Ibrahimo's story pointed up how misunderstanding can turn into suspicion, and hate.

In the same way the most innocent, even commendable actions (properly understood), can give rise to suspicion, fear and hatred. There was a common belief in a rather remote part of the Congo, in the last year of Belgian rule, that the large and excellent hospital at Bunia, some three hundred miles away, was in fact a slaughterhouse where African undesirables were eliminated by the doctors. Stories circulated about how a perfectly healthy person would be sent to the hospital, against his will, and would never come out again. Not even his body would be seen. The doctors, the story invariably went, injected the healthy individual with a powerful medicine that made him grow fat. Then when he was sufficiently succulent he was carved up and eaten. In this way the white doctors (and in the local language the same word meant "witch doctor") not only disposed of their enemies, but gained magical control over the souls of the dead Africans and could so bewitch the living. This, coupled with the cannibalistic Christian ritual of eating the flesh and drinking the blood of their ancestor, made the white man look even more sinister and evil.

The phenomenal ability of a few white men to assert authority over so many Africans is an indication, to the rural African, that the white man possesses powerful magic and is in league with powerful spirits. Witchcraft and sorcery are not the exotic things in Africa that they are to us; they are perfectly practical, understandable forces that can be wielded, to some extent, by almost anyone. Where this belief is as strong and as dominant as it is in many parts of Central Africa it provides a natural explanation for the white man's power. Even his skin color is taken as additional evidence, for white is the color commonly attributed to death, and it is used by the living, who smear their bodies with white clay during any festivals associated with death. So the white man's actions are not thought of as being merely hostile and aggressive; some much deeper and more sinister significance is attached to them. Thus Kithuica's conviction and execution might well have been thought of as being a deliberate attempt to make a blood feud inevitable, so providing the kind of dissension that destroys not only tribal living but also destroys the possibility of effective opposition to the administration.

Administrative and mission discouragement of some rituals and their prohibition of others only confirms this suspicion, and the African, forced to believe that the white man's magic is more powerful than his own because the white man *is* more powerful, comes to believe that the white man's success is almost inevitable. Once they suspect, as did Ibrahimo, that conversion to Christianity is a plot to prevent them from joining their own ancestors, at the same time giving them no place in the white man's afterworld any more than it does in the white man's world here and now, they begin to believe that the plot has succeeded. They realize that they are not only cut off from their unconverted relatives, at the same time being denied admission to the society of white men in this life, but that they will be equally isolated after death. The only alternative explanation is that they are destined to be the white man's slaves in the afterworld just as they are in this.

In the cities the African has been consistently taught to be ashamed of his tribal past and his religious beliefs, taught that he was a savage and a sinner, and often he has not learned otherwise. Nor has his attempt to become a black-skinned white man met with much success. In rural areas those who are not converted, either to Christianity or to a belief that the new world of the white man is the ideal to strive after, are little better off. Their faith in the old is shaken by the demonstrably superior power of the new, and insofar as it is made impossible for them to perform all the secular and ritual activities that are considered pleasing to the ancestors they feel that their life in the afterworld is likely to be equally unsuccessful and unpleasing.

Individuals find their own solutions to the dilemma, but the basic solidarity has been broken. Administrators tend to say that detribalization is a good thing, but they are thinking only in terms of administrative convenience. Detribalization brings with it the complete breakdown of moral and spiritual values, and separates each individual from his fellows. Under a strong central colonial government unity and conformity may be maintained—only by force. That is why the leaders of some new African nations, such as Nkrumah, feel that they also have to be a strong central power, ruling by force, as the only way to prevent disintegration. They are usually less, and certainly no more dictatorial than were the former colonial governments.

What is needed to restore an inner stability through which African societies can function themselves without the pressure of external force is the restoration of a common sense of values. Insofar as tribalism has broken down in urban areas it should be possible to develop a national sense, but there is no way of achieving this in rural areas except through many years of extensive and intensive education designed to break down tribal barriers and develop a wider sense of unity and a common system of values. The prospects of this being achieved are, at the moment, bleak. Schools are far too few and they are understaffed. Few of the African nations have the wealth or the qualified manpower to undertake the kind of edu-

cational program that is needed. The alternative is to continue ruling by force through a strong central government, which, as far as
rural areas are concerned, will just be another form of colonialism.

But perhaps even more important than the education of millions
of people from a tribal consciousness into a national consciousness is
the achievement, somehow, of a common sense of moral and spiritual values. At the moment there are two major formal religions in
Africa, Islam and Christianity, each mutually exclusive and hostile,
and the vast mass of so-called pagan beliefs, or tribal religions. Each
one of the latter, in its own context, is as successful as, if not
more so than, the two formal religions in achieving the same ends
of inner stability, but the present trends all make for a lessening of
their strength. Their destruction would mean the destruction of all
morality, of all inner incentive to live reasonably, fully and well.
Neither Islam nor Christianity could hope to fill the void that
would be left in time to prevent this catastrophe, yet both are
jointly declared enemies of paganism, and seek its destruction.

Wiser men, such as old Matungi, the traditional headman of
Ndola, and one or two missionaries who still seem to understand
that their religion is one of love, see no reason why all could not
exist side by side, growing in strength and unity through understanding. Most tribal Africans have the same wisdom and acknowledge honesty and goodness wherever they see it, once the tribal horizons are widened. It is perhaps the one chance the Africans have
of evolving a way of life and thought that will be their own, that
will be a source of unity and pride, that will be different from their
old tribal life, and different from the way of western civilization,
but that will still be perfectly compatible with the world all around
them, adding to it and enriching it. This is their only chance of
avoiding a long period of spiritual emptiness, and then we might
learn by their example what we should already have learned—that
goodness and truth and all the other virtues to which we pay lip
service are not the monopoly of our own particular world and way.

12

Lukamba

"I was one of the last real people to be born to my tribe. I was born in a world that was not good and was not bad, but it was more good than bad. There were other tribes around us that wanted to kill us because they wanted our land, but that was only because there were still others who wanted their land. We were powerful, and nobody conquered us, and we lived on between the two great rivers. Then the white man came and stopped all the fighting, and this was a good thing.

When I grew strong and my loins longed for women I was told that I had been chosen to enter the secret society of the Anyota, the leopard men. I was very frightened, because everyone knows that these leopard men eat human flesh, and I did not want to eat human flesh. But it was considered a great honor to be chosen, and in any case I could not refuse. I was bound by the strongest oaths not to say anything to anyone until after I had undergone trials. And so I became a leopard man, and was said to have been braver than any other before me. When it was all over men would look at the scars on my stomach and would say how great I must have been to live after such a terrible mauling from a leopard, but of course they knew that it was the Anyota who had scarred me in the manner of a leopard. I was proud and happy, for I had learned many things and knew that the Anyota was more than just eating of human flesh. It did not taste bad anyway. I was proud and happy because I knew that one day the safety of my people might be placed in my hands, because I was a man.

Shortly afterwards we heard that we all had to put on cloth and cover our stomachs, and we did not understand why. Then white men came with their guns and ripped the cloths off us and took all of us who carried the marks of the leopard away to their town. My father stayed by my side as long as he could, and I remember that before he was taken away from me he looked very sad and said: 'Try to live, Lukamba; you are young and they may spare you. But never forget your oath, and remember that you are a man.' I never saw him again, but I was told that the next day he was taken out and tied up with a rope around his neck. All those that were taken from our village were killed in this way, because the white men said the marks on our stomachs were evil and meant that we were murderers. So everyone with the marks had to be killed. I was sorry that my father died this way, he was a good man. I was not even allowed to see his body or to take it home to be buried. Even now I do not know where it is, but dying with so many other good men he will surely have been welcomed by the ancestors.

I was asked how old I was, and I said that I had become a man that year. They asked me if I had ever killed anyone, and I said no. They asked me if I had eaten human flesh, and I did not tell them the truth because the truth was not for them to hear . . . I said no. Then they told me that because I was so young and had not yet killed and eaten human beings they would not hang me, but I would have to go to live at a mission school and become a Christian. I thought this was a very good idea, and so I went to school.

At the school I learned many things, though they would not teach us to read, write, or to speak French; these things I had to learn from other people. This was a great pity because it would have been good to have understood what the white men said when they talked among themselves, or to have been able to talk to those who did not know my language. They taught us to recite passages from the Big Book, and when we had learned them they put water on our heads and said we were now Christians and when we died we would go to join the tribe of Bwana Yesu, who was a sort of blood father to all who went through the water initiation. This frightened some, because they did not want to think about death, and they certainly did not want to go anywhere except where their own fathers had gone. We were told that our fathers had gone elsewhere because they were evil. But I told the others not to worry, that it was all nonsense. I had read a great deal of the Big Book and it was plainly just a children's tale, such as one child tells to another. I was not tricked by it, although our teachers insisted that it was true.

At the Mission I also learned to work with wood, and how to make houses of wood, like those the white men lived in before they made bricks, and how to make tables and chairs and many other things. When I finished my schooling they kept me on as a carpenter and they even let me teach other boys. But when they learned that I was telling all the boys that the Big Book was just a children's story they told me I had to leave. I tried to explain that if I had not told the children that they would have been frightened and would not have wanted to be Christians, whereas there was nothing wrong with being a Christian, and the Big Book told very good stories, with much truth in them. I was sorry when they insisted that I leave because I had hoped eventually to be initiated into their secret society in which they eat human flesh, just as we do in the Anyota. It seemed strange that they should have been so angry about a custom that was so like their own.

But I got a good job with the white man who married a Bafwamiti girl. His name was Bwana Banduki, and he was a very good friend. But I did not sleep with his wife, as some said. I had my own wife, and had no need of other men's wives. I was made the head carpenter for the station, and had others working under me. None were from my own tribe, except my wife, but it was a good job. Bwana Banduki was not like other white men. He knew and understood our ways, and he spoke four or five of our languages.

We brought him all our disputes rather than go to the government tribunal, because he was able to decide well and he did not send anyone away to be put in a box unless they were very bad indeed, and even then he called us all and asked us first if we agreed with him that so-and-so should be put in a box.

Bwana Banduki also got the administration to give us a dispensary and he himself had a house built that could be used as a hospital. He even tried to start a school, but the teacher was always drunk and it was a bad thing for the children, so Bwana Banduki sent the teacher away. I and another from a different mission school did what we could, and Bwana Banduki paid us for this, though we did not ask it. If all white men were like him it would be a good thing. But other white men came to the station and spoiled everything. I think they did not like Bwana Banduki's having a black wife, and they certainly did not like the way he spoke to us, like one man to another, as equals.

These new white men made Bwana Banduki very unhappy, and they made his wife unhappy, and were the cause of much trouble between them. They turned the BaSinga of the next village against the Bwana, and against me because I was also a foreigner and a friend of the Bwana. And then they made a tree fall and kill the Bwana's child while it was still in his wife's stomach. Others said that it was Matungi, the witch doctor, but I never heard Matungi say anything against Bwana Banduki. The white man had given the orders for the cutting of the tree, and he caused it to fall as Safini was returning from Ndola with my wife. My wife told me all about it, and she was sure it was the white man's magic. Bwana Banduki said it was just an accident, but things like that do not happen unless somebody wants them to happen.

Things went very badly between the Bwana and his wife after that, and it was all part of this same curse. You could see it in the way the other white people laughed among themselves while they looked in the direction of the Bwana's house. This surprised me, because these people had been very good to me when I had told them that I was a Christian. But the Bwana used to say he was not a Christian, and this seemed more important than the fact that he was white, and the other white men were better toward me than they were to him. But when they started asking me about my friendship with the Bwana's wife I saw that they only wanted to make trouble, so I did not speak to them again.

I was very upset at the way these white people behaved towards the Bwana, and I decided to have nothing more to do with any of them, not even to listen to them, for all their words seemed to be lies. I thought a great deal about them, and began to listen to the talk I had ignored among my own people, about how the white man only wants to make us his slaves. I had always been angry at such talk, and pointed to Bwana Banduki as an example; but they said he was not typical, he had been entered by the spirits of a dead man of the Bafwamiti tribe, that was why he had had himself circumcised according to their rites. I mentioned the missions, and what good schools they had, but apparently the Mission near this village was not like mine, and had done very bad things. And it was true that there were many different kinds of Christians, who did not even talk to each other and who spoke of each other as though they were enemies. They only talked with one tongue when they talked against us instead of against each other.

I thought of the Mission where I had been, and how angry they had been with me for saying that their Big Book was a children's story. They must have thought us very stupid to expect otherwise, for even the greatest of our witch doctors can not walk on water, or make a great deal of food out of a little. Then I began to think they wanted to keep us in ignorance, for their ways were not as their words. They were men of great wealth, owning many motor cars and living in splendid houses with as much food as they could eat. They were eating all day long, not like us who eat only once, sometimes twice if we are lucky, in a day. Even at night, when it was dark, they sat around eating and drinking. Even though they told us to call them all Father, they did not treat us as though we were their own children, we were not one family. I do not even think they were our friends, and I do not know why they taught us so many good things, unless they were paid well. But who would pay them to teach us and why? I am told that they taught us because the white man needs us to do certain things, and for this reason he teaches us how to do them well. If they asked a white man to do them they would have to pay him many times what they pay us. But most of all I knew they were not our friends when they would not even talk with us about our own customs, and just told us that we must forget them and never remember them again. To take a man away from the ways of his fathers is very bad, and if we disrespect our own fathers, how can we respect him who asks us to call him Father?

It was some time before the curse that killed Safini's child that her friends left and went back to their village, for fear that some evil thing would happen to them. After that Safini, my wife and I were the only foreigners among the BaSinga, apart from Bwana Banduki, who was really of the Bafwamiti. And about this time we began to get new visitors to the Station, from Stanleyville. They were not of one tribe, but of many. They would not stay long, but for a night or two, then move on. They told us many things about the doings of the white man in Stanleyville, and how evil they were, wanting to makes slaves of us all. These men belonged to a new society called the Kitawala. It was formed after the Anyota was outlawed and it had recently been gaining much strength. They said that the white man had destroyed the Anyota, and other societies like it, and had destroyed our customs, because they wanted to destroy us. They said that the big hospitals in Stanleyville and Bunia, where black men went to be cured, were centers of sorcery where the white men killed the black man and ate his vitals so that he became black, and could come among us and spy on us and do us harm. Those who were kept alive were put into trances, sleeping strange sleeps, so that when they came awake they were unable to do anything except at the white man's bidding.

These men told us that the Kitawala was organized to break the power of the white man. They said that they followed ancient customs taught them by the witch doctors of many tribes, and had powers that were even greater and stronger than those of our own enemies. One was the ability to change the color of their skins at nighttime, so that they became white. Then as white men they were able to go to the big hotels in Stanleyville and eat big meals and drink much wine, and then just sign a magic piece of paper, like real white men, instead of paying. Sometimes they would sign paper and get money instead of food. But in the morning they would be black again, and when the white men brought the pieces of paper to the bank they would be told that no such person existed, and they would know they had been visited by the Kitawala. They would lose vast sums of money in this way, and they would become even poorer than the black man.

Another power the Kitawala had was the power to jump high in the air. This is how they were never caught, for even if they were surrounded they were able to jump high over the heads of their enemies, over the top of a house even, and escape. Sometimes they killed white men that had been particularly bad, and they always escaped in this way, leaving no footprints that could be followed.

I thought that the Kitawala was doing a good thing in cheating the white men just as they cheated us, but I did not like the idea of so many killings. Sometimes they killed innocent people too, though always it was claimed that the victims had witchcraft in their bellies. And I did not think it good to mix the ways of so many different tribes. Each of us should follow our own ways in peace, for this is pleasing to our fathers. To do otherwise is displeasing, and to use the powers of witch doctors for one's own gain is truly evil. Many of the Kitawala were growing fat on their powers, but it was not doing their fellows any good, nor was it doing any injury to the white men, who were as strong as ever.

They told me that I should join and for a long time I thought about it. They told me that it was like the Anyota, and reminded me of my vows. They told me that the white man had said he had come to help us, but he had done nothing that we could not have done ourselves, and he had taken all the gains for himself. This was true, and I thought I should at least give them a hearing. They did not have many members from the villages around about, but there were several at the Station, and others at the village of the big BaSinga chief, near Matadi. We used to meet there and report on all the white men we knew and what they were doing and how they behaved toward us.

But two things angered me. One was that it turned out that they did not have the magical powers they claimed at all. They merely talked that way in front of village people to impress them. In fact, coming from the city they had no knowledge even of their own tribal ways, let alone of anyone else's. But they used their reputation as sorcerers to force villagers to join the Kitawala, out of fear. And if they did not join they had them poisoned.

The other thing was that they did not want to regain the ways of the ancestors, to do away with the white man so that we could live once more the way we were meant to live; they only wanted it so that they could have more power over all of us. Anyone who joined had to do terrible things, and I was told that I would have to kill someone at the Station who had reported them to the administrator. I said I would do no such thing, but that if they liked I would tell Bwana Banduki and see what he said. They were shocked at this, and said that I must have nothing to do with the Bwana because he was white. I argued, but they said it made no difference, all white men were evil and would ultimately be killed or driven out. Again they reminded me of the scars on my stomach, and of my oaths to the Anyota. It was then that I decided to have no more to do with the Kitawala, and I told them so. At this they threatened me, but I opened my shirt and showed them the scars. I told them to think well before they killed a real man. I asked them where *their* scars were, and they had none. I told them that if they killed me all my people would rise up against them, and they did not like this because many of my tribe belonged to the Kitawala. Now I was ashamed of them, but I did not show it. I told them that I would leave, and so long as they did not trouble me I would tell no one who they were. They still hoped that I would join them later, so they let me go. One day they may try to kill me, for they know I do not like their ways.

I left with a bad heart because I had thought I would find men who believed in the ways of our ancestors, but instead I found only men who abused their fathers and wanted power and wealth for themselves. I had thought that the Kitawala would bring back to life the ways of the past, ways that are now nearly dead, but it only wanted to use the past to create new ways that were even worse than those of the white man. When I was a child I was taught that it was good to follow the old ways, and not the new. But I was not taught to hate the new, and to kill those who brought them. I was taught that the old ways were good because our ancestors discovered long ago how men should behave towards each other, as reasonable men—men whose heads did not turn in circles. Since then we have always behaved according to these ways, and we have grown strong in number. We do not lie to each other, we do not steal from each other, we do not sleep with each other's wives, and we do not kill each other. We live in peace. If strangers come to us we accept them in peace, unless they prove to be our enemies. We take them in as our friends, even as members of our families. Sometimes they stay with us and marry with us, and bring us more children, to whom we give our names. Others we leave to live their own lives, we do not call them good or bad.

The white man had other ways, but his ways we do say are bad, because they are not the ways of reasonable men. They lie and steal and cheat and kill and sleep with other men's wives, even among themselves. And all the time their mouths say it is evil for us to do these things, we who do *not* do them. And they do not accept strangers as friends, for to the white man all strangers are enemies, to be conquered, made slaves, or killed. We have conquered in the past, when we were forced to find new land for our growing people, but the white man conquers when he does not even need the land, he is already fat and well fed. He conquers for power. The administrators defeat our bodies, and the men of God defeat our hearts, we are left as nothing. At least when we conquered other people we took them and made them as ourselves.

The Kitawala is imitating the way of the white man, and it is no better because it is no more reasonable. The Kitawala say that they are only doing what the Anyota did, but this is not so. The Kitawala are fighting, the Anyota did not fight. The Kitawala kill to get rid of their enemies, they choose their victims; the Anyota killed only to preserve life, and only God knew who the victims were to be. My own brother was such a victim, but I still think the Anyota was a good thing. The white men do not understand it, neither do the Kitawala. Before I was cut and scarred I was a child, and I was frightened like a child. But when it was over I was a man, and knew how to behave to other men. At the Mission they told me the Anyota was savage and they beat me when I said it was beautiful. But it *was* beautiful.

I was taken from my home one morning, before my mother was awake. My father came with me. Then the man, who had first approached me about it, met us and took me from my father and walked me into the forest, far away. We were alone. He said he was my guardian, and he would try to help me as much as possible, but beyond a certain point he could not help, I would have to be my own guard. The forest was very silent, and I was scared. Then we came to a small clearing, and I was made to sit on a log with my back up against a tree. As I sat there he talked to me of death, and asked me if I was afraid. I said I was, and he slapped me, so I said I was not. He hit me with a stick until I began to cry, then he hit me harder until I stopped. Then he put my hands on my knees, straight out in front of me, and told me never to cry, and never to be afraid. He told me to remember that this was the way of the ancestors, and this was good. He said he was going away to urinate and would come back, but meanwhile I was not to move. I asked him why he did not urinate there, and he said it was a sacred place, he had to go elsewhere. Then he disappeared and I was left sitting with my back against the tree.

I was alone for an hour, and all the time I was listening for the return of my guardian. He had said he would help me and he had done nothing but hit and beat me. But when I caught myself feeling afraid I remembered how he had told me not to fear. And when I heard strange noises and wanted to cry out, I remembered he had beaten me until I had stopped crying. The forest was full of bad noises but I began to feel a little stronger, and very hungry. Then I heard it . . . the animal . . . the leopard.

If I could have cried I would have, but I had no voice in my throat. All my saliva turned to urine and I urinated in my bark cloth. My hands were still on my knees, and I found I could not move them. There was a rustling as the leopard came closer, and I could see the branches move and hear its snuffling breath. I thought that they had left me as food for the sacred leopard. I heard it move all around the clearing, thinking it might be a trap, and if I could have run I would have, but my hands were still fixed to my knees, and my feet would not move from the ground. I caught sight of the animal, its yellow and black skin shining for a moment in the sunlight. I had never seen a leopard so close before, and I tried hard to stare at it to make it think I was not afraid so that it would become scared and leave. But all of a sudden it moved again—I thought it was going to spring, but instead it slowly rose up on its hind legs and started walking toward me. Then I saw that it was not a leopard but a man inside a leopard's skin. His head was covered by the skin of a leopard's head, and his eyes shone through the holes where the leopard's eyes had been. Instead of claws there were great metal talons, and with these he reached out for my throat as he suddenly sprang off the ground, snarling, straight at me. I wanted to scream and to cry and to run away, but I could do none of these things, even, since my guardian had beaten me and told me not to. I thought I was to be killed, and I remember wishing only that it had been a real leopard. The terrible man-leopard seemed to jump right up in the air and he came down on top of me, his claws cutting my sides. I felt myself being lifted and carried away, and there was a horrible smell, I was put on the ground once more, and I saw the man-leopard stand over me, his eyes staring into mine, his claws again coming for my throat. I felt a cry coming, and I tried to hold it back so that at least I would die a man. But it came on, right from my stomach, as though it was pulling all my entrails out. It was loud and it frightened me, because it did not sound like a cry, it sounded like a laugh. Then I was as if dead—all was darkness except that in the darkness I could see those two eyes staring into mine.

When I woke up I was back in the clearing, with my back against the tree, and my guardian was holding my hands, which were still on my knees. He asked me what had happened, and he told me I had dreamed. I showed him the marks on my body where I had been torn by the claws. He asked me to describe the animal, and when I said it was a man-leopard, he said there was no such thing, it must have either been a man or a leopard. I told him it was neither, for no man would behave like that, and if it had been a leopard it would have killed me. He asked me again if I was sure that it was not a man, and I said yes. It was then I heard the sound again. This time there was no waiting, though. The undergrowth trembled and out came the man-leopard, walking up-

right and boldly. He stopped in front of me, and said in a voice
made strange by the mask over his face, 'You have proven yourself once, showing yourself free of fear. You did well when you
laughed. If you had been afraid I would have had to kill you, so
that you would not tell our secret to anyone. There is no turning
back. Now you have to prove yourself again and show me your
eyes.' He nodded to my guardian, who motioned me to lie down
on the ground. He then knelt at my head, while the man-leopard
stood astride my body, his eyes holding mine through the mask.
They were not human eyes, they were leopard eyes, and I could
not look away. He moved his right hand in front of my face so
that I saw the metal claws it held. I heard his throat rumble like
an angry leopard who had been disturbed, and the hand and the
claws went out of my sight . . . all I could see were the leopard
eyes, and all I could hear was the leopard noise, and all I could
smell was the leopard smell.

I felt the cold metal touch lightly on my stomach. It pressed
harder until it pierced the skin and I felt the warm blood trickle
down my side. Then the pain moved slowly across my stomach,
burning me all the way, like fire. The fire spread across my stomach
until it covered it from side to side, from my navel to my chest.
But the man-leopard's eyes held mine firmly, and kept them from
closing in pain. To shut your eyes on a leopard, they say, is death,
and I knew that my life was in my eyes.

I do not know how long it took, but when the cutting was finished the man-leopard at last took his eyes away and bent down,
putting his face to my belly. He must have been chewing some
forest plants, because from his mouth he sprayed a liquid onto the
wounds and with his hands rubbed it hard into the flesh below the
skin. The pain was a thousand times worse than the cutting, and
again his eyes sought mine and held them. My body was so weak
that even my hands could not protest, but lay at my side filled
with grass and earth, cut and bruised. My legs had no feelings in

them, and my guardian was holding my head. When the man-leopard finished rubbing the burning liquid into my wounds, my guardian put his hands over my face and closed my eyes, saying, 'You have done well, sleep.'

It was as though I had not slept for days. I remembered no more until I woke up in the late afternoon. I was still in the same clearing, and my guardian was with me. My stomach hurt terribly, and looking down I saw that the blood had dried, showing where the cuts lay, deep, like the gashes made by the claws of a leopard. It was as though a leopard had caught me from behind, its claws reaching around and tearing the flesh back on each side, several times. My guardian said to me: 'When people ask you what happened, you must say only, "A leopard caught me." Now it is time for you to know why.' He called out softly, and a man appeared, carrying a bundle wrapped in a cloth. It was Nyange, a highly respected man in our village, and whom I called Father.

He sat down beside me and talked. I knew that it was his voice I had heard behind the mask, but now it was kind and gentle, and I was no longer afraid.

Nyange told me that I was now a member of the Anyota, and that it had been necessary for me to prove my strength because the Anyota was a very powerful thing that needed only the strongest of men. I was told that it was a terrible thing, but that it was good. It was good because without the Anyota the tribe could not survive, and it was terrible because at times it had to kill. 'Just as I would have had to have killed you if you had not been strong,' said Nyange, 'just as a leopard kills. . . .'

He then unfastened the bundle at his side. First he took out the skin of a leopard. He threw this over his back, and my guardian helped to fasten the feet of the leopard to Nyange's arms and legs. The tail was held out by a piece of vine, and the skin of the head was pulled over Nyange's face. But he pushed it back so that he could talk more easily. He said that sometimes they used bark cloth painted to look like leopard skin, and he showed me how his body had been daubed with white clay to make it look like the spotted skin of the leopard. Next he picked up the metal claws which he fastened to his wrists, so that when he clenched his fingers the claws stood out over his knuckles. On one side of his belt he fastened a heavy knife, and on the other side he hung a wooden club, one end of which was fashioned in the shape of a leopard's foot.

He said: 'Sometimes there are great disputes among our people, disputes that do not settle themselves the way they should. When this happens our whole people divide in two, each taking one side or the other, and then we are weak, and our enemies fall upon us. Such a dispute is so bad that no man can settle it, so we, the Anyota, call on our ancestors. As men we can not speak with them, nor they with us. So we become one with the leopard, the master of death. Death comes to us in strange ways. It comes to young or old, good or bad, man or woman. There is no reason in its choice. In such a way does the leopard kill; swiftly and silently, returning unseen just as it comes unseen. By becoming one with the leopard we also become masters of death, and then we can speak with the ancestors. It is then that they talk to us and tell us what to do to make things come right with our people. They fill us with the power and the wisdom of the leopard, and they give us its speed and its silence and its strength, and they give us its hunger for flesh. We wait, as does the leopard, and we kill, as does the leopard. We do not know whom we kill, for we see only as the leopard, not as Nyange or as Lukamba. And after we have killed we eat part of the body, again like the leopard, leaving the rest to be found so that it will be known that the ancestors are angry and have commanded the Anyota to kill. We kill with our claws, piercing the neck, and we eat with our teeth, and when we are done, we leave the marks of the leopard's feet with this stick.'

Nyange waved his hands in front of me, showing how the claws would reach at each side of my throat, and he took his wooden stick and pressed it into the ground all around me, showing how it left the marks of a leopard's feet. 'After it is all done we go away and often we are sick, and when we wake up we do not know what we have done. But we know, as does the whole village, that the ancestors are angry and have commanded the Anyota to kill, and we know that the killings will go on until the fighting among ourselves is ended. We know that the Anyota does not choose its victims; death can come to anyone. You know this, Lukamba, for it came to your own brother that way, and perhaps that is why you and I and all the others are still alive. It was a good death, for your brother has surely gone to the ancestors, and we are left to do their will. Had your brother not died perhaps we would have continued to fight among ourselves and our enemies would have come and killed us all.'

Nyange then showed me many things. He showed me how I would have to learn to move about as does the leopard, how to make noises like the leopard. He showed me how to wait on the branch of a tree for a victim to pass, and then jump from behind, cutting his neck with the claws. In the days that followed I learned to do these things myself. Nyange called it 'learning to dance like the leopard.' It was a beautiful dance, and it made me feel good, for it made me feel close to the ancestors. I also learned how to kill and how to eat human flesh, and even this was beautiful, because it was the will of the ancestors. I did not like it at first, and I felt bad whenever Nyange fastened the claws to my hands and taught me how to jump on a victim, although I did not actually kill.

But Nyange taught me many other things as well. He told me many things I had not known about our ancestors, and their ways; about how they had come to this place a long time ago, and had grown and multiplied and made life possible for us, their children. They had learned how to live properly, and if we wanted to continue to live we also had to live that way, for it was the only way.

Some people had tried changing the ways of the ancestors, but they had all died, as had those who had broken their laws.

I began to see how our life was really a good life, and I began to understand why we did certain good things in order not to offend the ancestors. I had always been told that I should not steal, and when I grew older that I should not sleep with other men's wives; that I should not curse my parents or my brothers, and that I should teach my children to respect me as I respected my fathers. I had accepted these things, just as I accepted that it was forbidden to eat certain foods, and commanded that we offer other foods to certain relatives on certain occasions. But I had not understood why we did these things. Now I understood that by doing these things we were living the life that our fathers had lived before us, and their fathers before them, and that our children would live the same life after us, and their children after them. In this way our life was one, the past and the future, even in death. I also learned to be grateful to our ancestors for having taught us so well, for having shown us the way to live like men, and not like savages who hunt wild animals and grow no food of their own, who have no villages but wander from place to place, killing each other as they kill the animals. And I learned how it is good to take in any guest, even if he is your enemy, and to show him kindness if he asks for your hospitality. For in this way one makes friends beyond the village and even beyond the tribe, and grows stronger.

Above all, I learned to feel close to the ancestors, and to know that we were one with them, although I still did not know where they lived or how. But when I put on the skin of the leopard and painted my body and became as a leopard, the ancestors talked to me, and I felt them all around me. I was never frightened at such times, but felt good.

This is what we have lost, what we have had taken away from us. Now it is forbidden for us to talk to our ancestors, the Anyota is no more so we can no longer learn their will or call on them for help. We no longer have any reason for living, because we have been forced away from the ways of our ancestors, and we lead other men's lives, not the lives of our fathers. I had hoped that the new ways would be good, but I do not see it. If people do not steal and do not sleep with each other's wives, it is not because it is against the way of their ancestors, but only because they are afraid of being made to pay money, or of being put in a box at Matadi. In their hearts they want to steal, and in their minds they sleep with whomever they want. We were always told that to do something with one's heart or mind was the same as doing it with the body. It is not like that with the new ways. With the new ways you can wish people harm in your mind, but if you do not do them harm with your body you are not punished. Under the ways of our ancestors it was not like this. An evil wish was as bad as an evil deed, and was punished by the same law, for we knew that as much harm can come through man's mind as through his body. So also, if a man did harm to another with his body, but could show that his mind was good, he was not punished; but today it is otherwise. We no longer can even see why we are expected to do this or not to do that.

I had hoped also that the Kitawala might bring back the old ways, but it was only an imitation of the new, and even more evil. Now I know that the old ways have gone forever, the ancestors have left us because we have left them. We are surrounded by evil men who want to steal our souls by deceiving us with false ancestors, and men who steal our bodies and force them to strange ways. When we live like this the ancestors can not approach us, and we can not approach them, and we can only grow further apart.

If I try with my heart and my mind to live as I know I should live, honoring my fathers by trying to live their ways, perhaps I shall be claimed by them. I can do this, for I was taught. But today our villages are full of men and women who have never been taught, who have never been initiated into the secrets of their fathers and mothers, who only know of the Anyota the lies told by the white man. For them there is nothing. And because I am responsible for them, by these marks on my stomach, and because I can do nothing for them, being alone, I am afraid that for me too life afterwards, just like life here, will be empty. You white men have stolen our life from us forever."

Conclusion

To deal with all the present-day problems of transition in Africa would demand many volumes by many authors. Any attempt by a single author to compress the total problem into a single volume and to offer any single solution would result in gross superficiality, so here we have only attempted to see certain aspects of the overall question. There has been no pretense of a scientific analysis, but rather it is hoped that some insight may have been given into the African's point of view, and that some questions will have been raised in the reader's mind.

The chapters state a personal point of view with which the reader is not necessarily expected to agree; but each succeeding biography is fact, and from this body of fact anyone can draw his own conclusions. The total picture, as it emerges, may seem one-sided, and in a sense it is. There are quite enough apologists for the colonial cause. The purpose here is to show the attitudes of at least some Africans. The book at times may seem to be negative or to imply that western civilization has brought nothing but harm. This is unintentional, and no suggestion is meant that Africa would have been better left alone, or that the savage is necessarily noble. The chapters are intended to stimulate thought, even disagreement, and the biographies are there to supply food for that thought to feed upon. It is to the biographies that we should look for further information, for beneath apparently simple statements and actions lies a wealth of meaning, of thought and feeling. And it is to the biographies that we should look, each one of us, for light on the ultimate answer.

This raises the important question as to how representative the stories are. Each one concerns real people in real situations, though the names of the people and their villages have been changed and the exact location disguised. But Ndola is there, in the eastern part of the Congo Republic, and it is typical of that region, as are the stories of its inhabitants. There are plenty of problems that these particular villagers do not have, but that are of prime importance elsewhere. There is no industrialization near enough to Ndola to draw men away in large numbers, perhaps for several years, separating them from their families, leading inevitably to new situations such as widespread infidelity, divorce and, of course, wholesale prostitution. Ndola and its problems are, however, fairly representative of the enormous number of African villages that have to a large extent preserved a relatively traditional way of life and have had relatively little contact with the power that governs them from the outside. For the problem that confronts us here is the problem of tradition and its survival value.

In Africa, traditions and customs vary as widely as languages, and any scientific analysis would have to concern itself with specific societies. But there are certain general truths that emerge in the six simple biographies presented from Ndola, and from these we can, with due caution, draw some general conclusions. The first concerns the strength of tradition, the source and nature of that strength, and the narrowness—or breadth—of traditional horizons. Safini tells of her fears about going to live amongst the neighboring tribe, the BaSinga. She brought her friends to be with her, she would allow no BaSinga into her kitchen or to help her with any work that demanded any degree of intimacy. Yet when her friends, who shared her fear of the BaSinga but did not have the same bonds to hold them away from their home, decided to return to the Bafwamiti, then Safini allied herself all the more strongly with Lukamba and his wife, members of yet another tribe, but close to her because they were equally isolated in a foreign and hostile land. I happen to know Ndola and the Ba-Singa, and they are certainly not the ogres they were thought to be by Safini and Lukamba; this should be plain from the other biographies. But it is common in traditional African societies for one tribe consciously to maintain a feeling of separateness from its neighbors and to express it in terms of fear, mistrust, or even hostility. Sometimes the feeling has its basis in the historic fact of conquest or feud, but as often as not it expresses a strong desire to maintain separateness, to preserve tribal tradition intact, rather than any actual hostility. In this sense it is a kind of indigenous "apartheid"; but here it is practiced by mutual consent and desire, and it generally works efficiently enough unless some unavoidable pressures such as population growth and the need for territorial expansion force open hostility.

The strength of tribalism also shows in Lukamba's account of how he actually threatened the Kitawala, saying that if they killed him, his people, regardless of their strong support of the Kitawala, would retaliate. This indicates that even in a rampant nontraditional political organization such as the Kitawala, with a broad multitribal membership, tribal considerations and values play an important part, tribal loyalties come first.

Matungi's comments about the BaNgwana and the uncircumcised Zande, and even about the tribes closer to his own, show that from a ritual point of view they are considered unclean. Even Masoudi, hard pressed as he was to find a wife, eventually found one from his own tribe . . . "of course."

It is important to realize that this conscious sense of difference is one of opposition rather than of hostility. Matungi's attitude of live and let live is particularly significant. The fact that he considers the Zande unclean does not make him despise them, it merely formalizes a mutual exclusiveness at a ritual level. With this clearly established, there can then be satisfactory political contact, and there has been, in fact, a steadily increasing amount of economic contact. In fact it seems that the formalization of the difference at a ritual level is what makes successful contact possible at other levels, removing hostility and allowing each tradition to continue to flourish side by side with the other. It is when the difference is not formalized in this way that it is expressed through overt hostility.

It is possible, then, that there is here an unrecognized asset. "Tribalism" generally comes under fire from all sides without recognizing the force to unity that lies in the ability of tribal peoples to recognize the validity of other ways of life and thought in other people, rejecting them for themselves at the ritual level while co-operating at an economic or political level. "Detribalization" often involves a breakdown of values on all sides so that there is no longer the possibility for a relationship of difference to be formalized, and the result is hostility. It could be, then, that tribalism is of positive value and has something to offer toward the solution of the problem as to how to create nations out of tribes, how to reconcile one tradition with another, and all with the modern, western world. Many Africans see a justification of tribalism in the words of Christ: "In my Father's house are many mansions . . ." and when they hear us criticize tribalism without understanding it they point to our own exclusive nationalism and to our religious sectarianism and to our racism. And they see there, often enough, no mere formal differentiation, but a suspicion, contempt, bitterness, and thorough-going hatred that are by no means typical of tribalism. On the contrary, there is a curious spirit of tolerance that is as essential to tribalism as is the formal opposition, and we should weigh carefully the value of this against the alleged force of tribalism toward national disunity.

A tribe is generally too small a unit to survive alone in the modern economic and political world, but its existence does not in any way militate against a broader nationalism. It frequently forms a natural economic unit in the wider frame of reference, and it is clearly an administrative unit that can be dealt with as such. Any intertribal hostility that arises from other reasons can be controlled, just as can the reasons, by an indigenous central government, just as they have been controlled by colonial governments. And a central government consisting of members of voluntarily federated tribes is by no means foreign to Africa. In all parts of the continent there has been a constant history of powerful federations, built on the fact of tribalism rather than on its destruction. It has been said that the maintenance of tribal values militates against the development of national values. This is not necessarily so. There is obviously a need for common values, but this does not mean the inevitable destruction of the old, more local systems. One tribal member meeting another will trace his genealogy back far enough until he arrives at a common forefather, and he will know from that exactly how closely or how distantly he is related. He will also know exactly how to behave, for every degree of relationship carries its own responsibilities and privileges, and for each degree there is an appropriate system of behavior. Frequently a stranger will attach himself to a group, and the group is faced with the problem of how to formalize their relationship with him. They usually do it by inventing some fictitious relationship, so preserving the system through a known myth. Sometimes neighboring tribes who wish to co-operate more closely for one reason or another will unite by each extending their genealogies back a stage beyond the original ancestor, the founder of the tribe, and will create the myth that the two founders were actually brothers, thus uniting the two pyramidal organizations. This process can be extended *ad infinitum,* and could conceivably become one means of uniting many, if not all, tribes in any one national area. Each tribe would preserve its own identity and its

own values, the only values that make it the efficiently function-
ing, moral, law-abiding unit it is, yet each would have a common bond, recognizable in traditional terms, with the others.

At this point it should be mentioned that while throughout
the biographies there are references to ancestors and to afterlife,
such beliefs are not universal in Africa. There is no one common
system of values any more than there is a common economic or
political system. One of the major problems in Africa is its immense diversity. But a respect for the ways of the ancestors *is*
almost universal, and this respect encourages the desire to per-
petuate these ways in the belief that this will bring good fortune
in this life, if not in the next. There is an immediacy about the
remote past that is foreign to the western way of thought, and it
involves emotional attitudes that are no less strong if the belief
does not involve a stated notion that after death we go to join our
ancestors. In many cases beliefs exist in a general way, but are
not formulated clearly enough to be formalized in ritual or in
dogma. They may still constitute a powerful sanction of social
behavior, however, and invariably when they are interfered with,
such interference is accompanied by moral as well as spiritual
degeneration.

When we look at those peoples still largely living the traditional way of life, but in the security of enforced peace, we discover several significant facts. Firstly, in the absence of economic
pressures there is no desire even for a resumption of active hostility.
Internecine warfare is *not* a natural part of the make-up of African
tribes any more than it is of western nations, and in many cases it
is demonstrably less so, for there are formal ways specifically
designed to avoid armed conflict on a large scale and to resolve disputes with a minimum loss of life. This is a nice reversal of our
own political mechanisms, which attempt to avoid conflict by
preparing for annihilation and destruction on a scale incompre-

hensible to any "tribal" African, and with a singular premeditated brutality utterly unknown to him.

We have already mentioned that there are tribal oppositions that are consciously maintained, but the significant fact is that when contact or conflict is inevitable, the situation is resolved either through assimilation or through the system of indigenous "apartheid" to which we have referred. The strength of the latter system is that it allows each group to preserve its full identity and its full values, if anything mutually reinforcing each other's solidarity. Further, we have to try and understand that while Tribe A feels superior to Tribe B, it does not mean, even to a member of A, that Tribe B is inferior. It is merely a question of the relativity of points of view. There is no specific advantage of this kind of "apartheid" over assimilation; it depends largely on the distribution, density, and economies of the populations concerned, and whether or not the available land can support two economies that might perhaps be distinct and exclusive (nomadic pastoralism and settled cultivation).

Another trait of traditional societies is their adaptability, within recognizable limitations. The African tribe never has been static, with possible rare exceptions, and it owes its survival to its adaptability. It is not nearly as exclusive, either at the level of the tribe or that of the individual family, as is often imagined. Adoption of groups of strangers or of individual strangers is frequently considered a healthy and desirable practice, and there are social mechanisms for incorporating such strangers effectively and fully into the society. Similarly, customs are frequently borrowed and adapted, and this will in effect create mutual bonds where none existed before. They may be loose at first, but they will pave the way for eventual assimilation. The difficulties experienced in adaptation to the western way of life are not entirely due to the greatness of the difference, nor even to the speed with which the adaptation often has to be made, but rather they are due to the way in which the Europeans themselves have tried to guide or force this adaptation. The African is perfectly capable of taking what he wants and needs, and, even more important, he knows what he needs to retain of the old to preserve not only continuity but cohesion. This is a process that has to grow from within; any attempt to impose from outside is bound to be disastrous.

It is in the past that the tribe finds its present strength, its present cohesion, its present morality; and it can be seen in the biographies that morality is conceived of as being far above mere obedience to the letter of a written, police-enforced law. But more important still is that in the past the tribe finds the incentive to work for the future, and to maintain its present integrity. If the past is destroyed, through taught disbelief, or through exposure to scorn and ridicule, or because of the twisted, unperceptive "evidence" of science, the result can only be total collapse and chaos.

In the sense that the tribe is a vast, extended family, where every member stands in a definite relationship to every other, it is obviously very much a society, and not a mere conglomeration of individuals who happen to live in the same territory. Loyalty is felt in varying degrees—generally for one's immediate family, through them to one's lineage, then the clan, and then the tribe. But there are effective institutional ways of avoiding any family sectarianism, and of extending one's loyalties at a generational level beyond the lineage or clan. They may be guilds, secret societies or age-sets, but they indicate an awareness of the necessity for expanding one's social horizon and one's obligations and privileges in different directions simultaneously. The unity of a tribe is as secure as it is complex and tightly knit. It would be difficult to create such a unity on a national basis; the colonial powers, at all events, seem to have failed spectacularly enough.

The dangers lie more in detribalization, for this creates a hiatus and leaves lacunae that no concept of nationhood can fill overnight. And, because of this, the general degeneration of internal order and discipline calls for at least an interim government that cannot afford to be less than dictatorial. Such governments may well be necessary when colonial authorities withdraw without having educated and trained even a skeleton government to leave behind them; but once a dictatorship is established, however valid and benevolent it may have been at the outset, the tendency is for it to follow the all too familiar pattern.

The hope lies in an appreciation of the true, practical values of the past, of tradition, by the new leaders of Africa. Even in the blunt terms of political expediency, the past is of incalculable value. The leaders, unfortunately, are too often those who have been dazzled by the gaudy tinsel of western civilization, and who have been weaned away from tradition as though it were something wholly corrupt and evil. That the two worlds have to come to terms is certain, but this need involve the defeat of neither, though Africans in the past have accused the west of destroying their traditions and of failing to respect their right to live according to their own principles, and some are now clamoring for the destruction of the white man in Africa. But the balance at the moment is more delicate than ever, for the insidious assumption that the western way is all-powerful and therefore all-good has reached into every corner of the continent. The last strongholds of self-respect, of morality, of belief and faith, are threatened by the cheapest and most tawdry offerings that western technology can devise: a soul can be bought for a piece of printed cloth or for a packet of cigarettes. It would be ironical indeed if the ultimate act of destruction, so carefully if unconsciously prepared for by the colonial powers, should come from the Africans themselves through an ignorance of the immensity of their own heritage.

About the Author

COLIN M. TURNBULL was born in London, and now lives in Connecticut. He was educated at Westminster School and Magdalen College, Oxford, where he studied philosophy and politics. After serving in the Royal Naval Volunteer Reserve during World War II, he held a research grant for two years in the Department of Indian Religion and Philosophy, at Banaras Hindu University, in India, and then returned to Oxford, where he studied anthropology specializing in the African field.

He has made five extended field trips to Africa, the last of which was spent mainly in the Republic of Zaïre. From these trips he drew the material for his first book, *The Forest People*, an account of the three years he spent with the Pygmies of Zaïre.

Mr. Turnbull was a Professor of Anthropology at George Washington University in Washington, D.C. He is a Research Associate at the American Museum of Natural History, in New York, and a Corresponding Member of Le Musée Royale d'Afrique Centrale.